LULAC

THIS IS AMERICA!
As citizens we must make some
contribution to the American
Stream of Life. As members of
Lulac we must make that con-
tribution outstanding.
                Raoul A. Cortez

Cover of the *LULAC News*, Vol. 16, No. 4 (April 1950).

The Evolution of a Mexican

LULAC

American Political Organization

Benjamin Márquez

University of Texas Press, Austin

First edition, 1993

Requests for permission to reproduce material from this work should be sent to Permissions, University of Texas Press, Box 7819, Austin, TX 78713-7819.

∞ The paper used in this publication meets the minimum requirements of American National Standard for Information Sciences—Permanence of Paper for Printed Library Materials, ANSI Z39.48–1984.

All illustrations are from the Nettie Lee Benson Latin American Collection, General Libraries, The University of Texas at Austin. Used with permission.

Grateful acknowledgment is made to the following for permission to quote from copyrighted material.
    Social Science Journal: For material from Márquez, Benjamin, "Organizational Maintenance and the League of United Latin American Citizens." *Social Science Journal* 28, no. 2 (April 1991).
    Social Science Quarterly: For material from Márquez, Benjamin, "The Politics of Race and Class: The League of United Latin American Citizens in the Post–World War II Period." *Social Science Quarterly* 68, no. 1 (March 1987).
    Western Political Quarterly: For material from Márquez, Benjamin, "The Politics of Race and Assimilation." *Western Political Quarterly* 42, no. 2 (June 1989).

Library of Congress Cataloging-in-Publication Data

Márquez, Benjamin, date.
    LULAC : the evolution of a Mexican American political organization / Benjamin Márquez.—1st ed.
        p.   cm.
    Includes bibliographical references and index.
    ISBN 0-292-75154-0 (pbk.)
    ISBN 0-292-75152-4 (alk. paper)
    1. League of United Latin American Citizens.   2. Mexican Americans—Politics and government.   I. Title.
    E184.M5M357   1993
    322.4'089'6872073—DC20   92-28983

To Lolita, Carlos, Carina, and Antoñio

Contents

Photographs following page 60

Acknowledgments

During the course of writing this book, I have incurred many debts that I would like to acknowledge. The research began when I was a teaching fellow in the Department of Political Science at the University of Kansas. I am grateful for the research support provided by the University of Kansas Endowment Association and the University of Kansas Office of Academic Affairs. I am also grateful for the support of the National Endowment Association during the initial phases of that research.

I received the assistance of many individuals. I am grateful for the patient and thorough assistance of the librarians at the Benson Latin American Library at the University of Texas at Austin. Gilda Baeza, Jane Garner, Michael O. Hironymous, Anne Jordan, Carmen C. Sacomani, and Wanda Turnley helped me through the voluminous LULAC archives. César Caballero of the University of Texas at El Paso Library and Thomas Kreneck of the Houston Public Library helped direct me to rare LULAC documents in their special collections.

I owe a special thanks to my many colleagues who read the book in one of its many manifestations. Manuel Avalos of the University of Arizona, Rodolfo de la Garza of the University of Texas, and John García of the University of Arizona all offered helpful criticisms. Dalmas Nelson and John Francis at the University of Utah provided me with insights and moral support. I would also like to acknowledge the research assistance of Kenny Lawson and Edwin Olson. I am especially indebted to David Gutiérrez of the University of California–San Diego who took the time to read and criticize my work. Finally, I would like to thank all of the LULAC activists, past and present, who shared their memories and materials with me, including Lucy Acosta, Paul Andow, Albert Armendáriz, Ruben Bonilla, William Bonilla, José de Lara, Anita del Río,

John García, Paul Garza, Jr., Manuel González, Alfred J. Hernández, John J. Herrera, Edward Morga, Mario Obledo, Roberto Ornelas, Eduardo Peña, Frank Pinedo, Belén Robles, Luciano Santoscoy, and Pete Villa. Of course, any errors of fact or interpretation are mine alone.

LULAC

1. Introduction

This book is a study of a Mexican American middle-class political organization, the League of United Latin American Citizens (LULAC). Established in Corpus Christi, Texas, in 1929, the group has evolved into one of the most important of all Mexican American civil rights organizations. Representing the upwardly mobile sector of the Mexican American people, LULAC has fought to integrate its people into the American social and economic mainstream. Because of its commitment to American patriotism and advocacy of social assimilation, the group quickly gained a reputation for reformist tactics and goals. Although LULAC would stridently criticize American society for discriminating against Mexican Americans, it nonetheless tended to promote reform rather than a restructuring of the political or economic status quo. Its members cherished the ideals upon which the United States was founded; their writings and public statements were filled with praise for U.S. political institutions as well as the American system of free enterprise. While the organization challenged the hypocrisy of these same institutions and processes, its struggle to eliminate racial discrimination was designed to give Mexican Americans the opportunity to compete in the economic marketplace on an equal footing with Anglo Americans. LULAC's politics was that of assimilation and accommodation, with the major goal to reform American society and fit in with the white majority (E. Garza 1951; M. García 1984a; Sandoval 1979). Its political activities and philosophy have not only earned the group a central place in Mexican American political history, it continues to be the largest and most visible Latino organization in the United States. Active in minority political affairs since its inception, LULAC has evolved into one of the most important of all Mexican American civil rights organizations.

LULAC members were aggressive defenders of a people with

whom they identified and whom they believed were the target of pervasive and often violent discrimination. Very early in the group's history, LULAC established a record of fighting discrimination, often at great risk to its members' personal and physical well-being. For example, one activist recalled that in the early 1930s the LULAC Flying Squadrons, or organizing teams, were subject to harassment or arrest by law enforcement officials in South Texas who believed that LULAC represented a subversive force. From time to time the Texas Rangers would set up roadblocks in order to intercept LULAC organizers as they traveled from town to town (Herrera 1985).

LULAC's political platform incorporated a number of seemingly contradictory goals. These early activists were crusaders who fought racism with a religious zeal while embracing the country that rejected their people and culture. LULAC members maintained a pride in and sought to preserve their Mexican heritage while advocating the acquisition of the English language, loyalty to the United States, and participation in American civic and social activities. They were early advocates of bilingualism and biculturalism, as long as it was understood that the Mexican American's primary loyalty was to the United States and its institutions. Finally, the founders of LULAC were economic conservatives who saw racial discrimination, not class domination, as the primary cause of the Mexican American's problems. From the LULAC members' perspective, if prejudice could be done away with, little else in society needed changing. They believed that talent, ability, and fortitude were randomly distributed in any racial group, and those factors alone should determine an individual's social mobility.

The individuals who made up the organization came from communities where poverty and suffering were unavoidable facts of life (see de León 1989: Chap. 7). However, their prescriptions for social change sprang from a world view in which individual initiative and achievement were central, and where economic processes and class power were minimized or ignored. This set of beliefs remained relatively intact throughout LULAC's history. From the late 1920s to the 1990s LULAC's ideologists envisioned a just society as one which was free of the distortions produced by race prejudice, where a person's economic mobility was determined on the basis of individual merits, and where a capitalist economy reigned.

Throughout this historical analysis of LULAC and its integrationist politics, several key issues concerning minority group dynamics will be addressed. First, race and the role it plays in political mobilization, long a matter of concern for political scientists, will be examined in detail (Wolfinger 1965; Stone 1985; Preston et al. 1987). Race was a central concept to LULAC ideologists, and, consequently, the way they framed the problem and envisioned its solution had a profound impact on the organization's development and structure. Their two major mobilization periods, the late 1920s and the late 1940s, were times in which appeals were made to potential activists to work in the interests of mutual aid and protection. While tracing LULAC's evolution, the role that race played in its organizing and political struggles will be examined.

Second, political scientists and sociologists have documented the process by which minority groups are absorbed by a dominant culture and gradually lose their group distinctiveness (Gordon 1964; Lieberson 1980; Sowell 1981). LULAC represented an organization which sought to defend the Mexican American community's interests by pursuing a strategy of integration. The literature on race and ethnicity argues that as members of an ethnic minority achieve economic mobility, ethnic solidarity and cohesion begin to break down (Dahl 1961; Eisinger 1980). As a leading advocate of economic and cultural assimilation, LULAC's political program provides an excellent example of a political strategy that could lead to an eventual breakdown in group cohesiveness. Indeed, not only was its program likely to have such an effect, but the group argued that social and economic integration was its central political goal.

Finally, this work is a study in political ideology. There is a paucity of research on political organizations emerging from the Mexican American community, and the question of ideology has received little attention (Barrera 1985; Muñoz 1989). Early studies that documented the range of political goals and platforms within the Mexican American community were largely descriptive in their approach (Tirado 1970; Alvarez 1973). Few scholars have examined the economic background of group activists, their goals, strategies, and values (Barrera 1979; M. García 1989). A primary goal of this book is to examine these variables and understand the dynamics behind LULAC's singular interpretation of race and race relations. LULAC fought an uncompromising battle for racial equality while remaining economically conservative. Understanding LULAC's political ideology will allow us to assess the relative weight that class and ethnic origins played in forming a distinctive perspective among one segment of the Mexican American population. LULAC's political position concerning race and racism was part of an elaborate philosophy which valued free market capitalism and individual mobility. While LULAC was proposing to dismantle a harsh system of racism, its values were such that racism was virtually the only problem it identified as oppressing Mexican American people.

Organizing Framework and Data Sources

Much of the recent literature on political organizations has focused on the incentives necessary to induce individuals to join groups and support their goals over an extended period of time (Salisbury 1984). In this study, questions of race, group solidarity, and political ideology are posed within the perspective of LULAC's organizational development; that is, the relationship between the individual members and the organization's reward structure. The incentive theory literature helps us understand LULAC's evolution as an organization because it analyzes the individual's reasons for participation in an organization and the relationship between leaders and followers. The classic formulation of the paradigm was stated by Olson (1971), who argued that a group must provide rewards or incentives to its members in order to secure their commitment and participation. His most provocative assertion from the standpoint of self-interest is that it is "irrational" to take part in collective action. Individuals can usually benefit from an organization's achievements without having to contribute their own time and effort to realize a group's goals if nonmembers cannot be excluded from benefits derived from group achievements. Olson further argued that instances of collective action, not collective goods, result from selective incentives to individuals. In short, individuals are rational decision makers who will avoid group participation if they can enjoy the benefits of group actions without incurring any participation costs. When they do participate, it is only to enjoy individually consumable benefits provided by the organization.

More recent work in this field has modified the assertion that collective action is irrational and has paid more attention to the context of a given situation which might make group participation a rational enterprise. This interpretation of human behavior and organizational dynamics views individuals as rational decision makers who value selective rewards as well as collective goals. In this way, one can explain the apparent self-sacrificing or altruistic behavior of political activists and still account for their behavior as a rational calculation in which the benefits they derive exceed the cost of joining. While this interpretation argues that both types of incentives are important, individually consumable rewards are still the strongest and most reliable incentives organizations can offer their members. Individuals will join political organizations to achieve collective goals, but in order to keep them active over a long period of time, the group will have to provide selective rewards and incentives (Clark and Wilson 1961; Hansen 1985; V. K. Smith 1985).

This interpretation of collective behavior stands in contrast to another tradition which suggests that minority politics is different in respect to the efficacy of collective goals. Because racism is held to be a tenacious problem which affects all members of a racial group, minority organizations should be able to attract and retain members through appeals to altruism (Barrera 1985; Bayes 1982; Morris 1984). Because problems faced by minorities are so severe, the need to solve them is a pressing and lasting motivation to collective action. Moreover, according to this line of reasoning, racism can serve to motivate individuals in the absence of material benefits derived from group membership (Pinckney 1984: 110). However, if individuals are economic maximizers, the role that incentives play in the longevity and structure of organizations should be similar for all voluntary groups regardless of their original intent.

The types of incentives offered by an organization can help us understand not only why individuals choose to invest their time and effort in political activity, but also how a group can survive beyond its initial mobilization stage. There are three basic types of incentives: (1) material benefits (the tangible rewards of participation such as income or services that usually have monetary value); (2) solidary benefits (those socially derived rewards created by the act of association, such as fun, camaraderie, status, or prestige); and (3) purposive or expressive rewards (those derived from advocating a particular cause or ideological orientation). Incentive theory also argues that individuals will not contribute to group activity as long as they can reap the benefits of a group's efforts without joining. However, if nonparticipants can be excluded from the benefits generated through group membership, these three categories of rewards can serve as effective inducements (Cigler 1986; Salisbury 1969). From this perspective, the motor of group dynamics is an economic exchange in which members calculate the benefits of joining against the cost of participation. It is the job of leaders (or entrepreneurs) to develop incentives that will entice followers (or consumers) to join and participate.

The logic of incentive theory suggests that even minority organizations cannot rely on the existence of racism or group subordination to maintain a viable and active group. As groups mature, purposive rewards are likely to be less effective than solidary and material incentives, which must be relied on to generate member enthusiasm. Newly formed groups will rely almost exclusively on purposive incentives in order to maintain group cohesiveness; ideological expression and a sense of purpose will serve as rewards to their activists. But with the passage of time, even the most dedicated partisans will tire of and drift away from active group participation. If the group is to survive, the leadership will be forced to generate alternative incentives that are more reliable and economical, such as insurance policies, consumer goods with a group discount, or social and recreational activities. In the long run, a group must eventually provide its members with material and solidary rewards if it is to survive (Clark and Wilson 1961).

Cigler (1984) has suggested a two-stage scenario for understanding a group's change in incentive structure. In the first, or "mobilization," stage, a number of individuals identify a common problem to be addressed through collective action. A cadre of leaders is found who secure control over resources, develop strategies, and guide the group in actions designed to achieve those goals. The second phase involves bureaucratization. After the initial series of issues and events that originally sparked a group's formation have passed or are no longer pressing, a willingness to bear participation costs will decline. In this phase, the group becomes concerned with continuity and its survival will often depend on the leadership's ability to adapt incentives to a changing context. Often, the original goals are either forgotten or attended to in a perfunctory manner.

These claims have clear implications for organizations such as LULAC. In an early work on the development of civil rights organizations, Wilson (1973) noted that few protest groups were able to survive beyond their formative stages unless they were able to move away from an exclusive dependence on purposive benefits. Two dynamics can be observed in this process. First, the rank and file members will lose their enthusiasm for pursuing collective goals. They will find that the costs (time, effort, frustration, etc.) of continued participation outweigh the original or collective benefits. Second, a leadership core whose participation is maintained through prestige and satisfaction and is derived through its position within the group assumes responsibility for much of the group's everyday activities. In order to insure its survival, the group must develop a stable leadership hierarchy and reduce the burden of demands placed upon its members (Walker 1983). Incentive theory predicts activist organizations are destined to evolve into nonpolitical entities. As a result, rather than continuing to vigorously pursue the group's original goals, organizations such as LULAC are likely to become increasingly dependent upon outside financial support, and the direct participation and influence of its membership will be decreased as the maintenance of the organization per se becomes an all-encompassing goal (Cigler 1984, 1986).

This book analyzes LULAC's incentive structure and how it changed over time. From 1929 to the beginning of World War II and from 1945 to the early 1960s the group had an active membership base. In these periods, the LULAC rank and file was engaged in such activities as protest, petition drives, community education campaigns, and litigation in a crusade for equal civil rights for Mexican Americans. Over time, the group was transformed from a membership-based organization dealing in collective (purposive) benefits to a staff (or elite) organization dispensing solidary and symbolic rewards, in part because many of the members who joined the group during its mobilization stage felt LULAC had achieved its aims. For those who joined the group after World War II, all the purposive and expressive rewards LULAC offered had been dispensed by the early 1960s. The problem of waning membership enthusiasm was solved by drastically reducing participation costs and turning to the federal government and the private sector for funding. The central thesis of this book is that LULAC's longevity was due to the organization's ability to effectively adjust its incentive structure during the late 1960s and early 1970s. This change in the incentive structure transformed the organization from an activist civil rights group to a staff- or elite-dominated group that would devote much of its energies to continuity and survival.

This book will assess the empirical claims of exchange theory by analyzing the organizational transformation of LULAC. All the elements for a good case study of a group's incentive structure and its evolution over time are represented in the political activities of this seminal organization. If exchange theory has any explanatory value, the organization's incentive structure should change in a predictable manner. LULAC began as an organization offering purposive incentives; that is, social change in the form of equal rights for Mexican Americans. Members were called upon to participate out of a sense of justice or to receive a sense of satisfaction fighting the discrimination Mexican Americans had to endure in South Texas during the turn of the century. LULAC members might also receive material rewards in the form of life insurance policies, burial insurance, or the benefit of a credit union, as was the practice with the more traditional Mexican American *mutualistas* (mutual aid societies). Finally, LULAC members might receive material rewards in the form of employment through the organization or increased employment opportunities in society at large through its efforts to eliminate discrimination. However, as long as legal and de facto discrimination against people of Mexican origin remained strong, we could expect purposive and expressive rewards to define the relationship between LULAC and its followers.

As time passed and many of the barriers that prevented talented and ambitious Mexican Americans from achieving upward mobility were removed (partly as a result of LULAC's efforts), the group's incentive structure changed. Exchange theory assumes that at some point purposive and expressive incentives will lose their effectiveness over time as group members are likely to tire of the struggle or be distracted by other matters. In the face of continued failure to achieve a given goal or even if an organization's goals are realized, members will drift on to other concerns unless the exchange formula is renegotiated. At this point, any group is in danger of collapse unless the problem is recognized and corrective action taken. In the mid-1960s LULAC was faced with such a crisis. It was forced to adopt a new strategy in order to maintain a hold on its existing membership and reach out to a new generation of Mexican Americans. Incentive theory suggests that the most effective way to do this is to increase the group's material rewards and lighten the demands made upon the general membership. The number of social activities could be increased, dues lowered (or kept at a constant level), and the demands on the membership's time decreased. Finally, the group could solicit funds from outside sources in order to finance the new exchange formula.

Are minority organizations destined to evolve into nonpolitical entities whose membership's concerns center on material or solidary rewards? An analysis of LULAC's political history and ideological development will help draw some important lessons concerning minority political mobilization. First, although political organizations allow dispossessed groups to articulate issues and mobilize resources, the passage of time may work to erode their effectiveness. A decline in a group's ability to work for political goals could occur even if the group fails to achieve its original goals. Second, incentive theory suggests that individual self-interest is at war with ethnic loyalty and that in the long run the latter will yield to the former. If this is true, minority organizations will eventually adopt political goals and strategies beneficial to their members' economic interests regardless of any altruistic intent. Finally, if the goals of civil rights organizations like LULAC succeed in eliminating discriminatory practices against minorities, the need for racially based organizations will decline and class cleavages will assume a larger role in the minority community's politics.

On the face of it, LULAC appears to have avoided these pitfalls. Unlike many other Mexican American organizations, LULAC has displayed a remarkable longevity and has grown from a small network of councils in South Texas to one with active councils, or organizational units, in twenty-eight states, a national headquarters, and a professional staff.

One interpretation of the group's continued survival would be that LULAC has defied the expectations of the incentive theory literature and has continued to attract political activists from the community. In this scenario, the social and economic problems facing the Mexican American community and the possibility of doing something about them are the primary reasons activists rally around the LULAC banner. In short, purposive incentives might continue to play a central role in the group's rewards structure. On the other hand, if minority organizations are subject to the same pressures other groups are, other outcomes are possible. As long-time members tire of pursuing LULAC's original goals or those original goals seem irrelevant to changing circumstances, other Mexican American political organizations that offer new or more aggressive sets of purposive incentives may have usurped the political role that LULAC once played. These groups now siphon off the politically committed activists from the community. In this case LULAC, having lost out to other groups in the competition for politically committed members, will have to find other ways of surviving by offering material or solidary incentives to its members rather than committing them to continued political activity.

The Evolution of LULAC'S Incentive Structure

Founded at a time when race relations were worsening and the nation was moving into a depression, LULAC advocated change through socially sanctioned means and adopted a strongly patriotic stance. As its "Aims and Purposes" declared, its members were true and loyal citizens of the United States whose primary obligation was "to protect and promote the education of our people in accordance with the best American principles and standards." LULAC's members belonged to a racial and cultural minority group whose aims were to declare its loyalty to the United States, adopt American culture, and renounce any political loyalty to Mexico and its institutions. Furthermore, LULAC desired a society where discrimination was unknown and where economic rewards were decided by the invisible hand of the free market. Thus we find a clear set of organizing incentives promoted by a minority civil rights group in the late 1920s. How these principles acted as inducements for individuals to join the group and how their effectiveness changed over the years can provide some important insights into the functioning of minority political organizations.

These ideals set the tone for forty years of LULAC politics and, when closely scrutinized, allow us to understand the internal dynamics and survival tactics of this minority political organization. LULAC's political history is made more interesting by the fact that the group was a solidly conservative one.

Both as a result of the membership's political preferences and the need to placate a prejudiced and suspicious Anglo population, LULAC's ideology expressed a strong dedication to American institutions of government and free market capitalism. Officers and members of LULAC were required to take an oath swearing that they would be "loyal to the government of the United States of America, support its Constitution and obey its laws" (Sandoval 1979: 13). The organization would adopt "America" as its official song, English as its official language, and the "George Washington Prayer" as its official prayer (E. Garza 1951: 9, 18). The league's constitution was also modeled after the U.S. Constitution (Canales 1937: 34).

At the onset of World War II, many LULAC councils ceased to exist because their members volunteered or were drafted into the armed services. After World War II, the group was revived with an influx of returning veterans. These veterans constituted the core of activists who would renew the fight for equal civil rights. For fifteen years after the Second World War, the organization would conduct a series of lawsuits, petition local government, and mobilize the Mexican American vote in order to challenge discriminatory practices throughout the Southwest. Along with another group, the American GI Forum, LULAC was at the forefront of civil rights activism for Mexican Americans in the post–World War II period.

LULAC is unique from an organizational perspective partly because it experienced two mobilization stages, the first in 1929 when the group was founded, and the second in 1945 after World War II. The start of the Second World War disrupted LULAC's evolution, and most of its councils disbanded. However, after the war, returning Mexican American veterans revived the moribund organization and embarked on a membership drive. Thus, LULAC reorganized and the question of participation and the rewards derived through group membership could be studied anew. The period from 1945 to the late 1950s represented a long period of political activism, one in which members were motivated by an appeal to purposive and expressive rewards. This fifteen-year period was not without its strains. Toward the end of the 1950s ideology, political goals, and ethnic group solidarity lost much of their effectiveness as motivating forces and LULAC began to follow the pattern of organizational development predicted by incentive theory. A major source of this change stemmed from the fact that many of the members who joined the group after World War II felt that many of their objectives had been achieved. Membership began to drop and the once dynamic organization atrophied.

During the 1960s, new generations of leaders were able to save LULAC from dissolution not by reviving the activist spirit of existing membership but rather through the use of government- and corporate-sponsored programs to fund increased organizational activity. The proliferation of more radical political organizations during this period provided new outlets for Mexican American activists. LULAC was no longer the single most important organization in the community. Indeed, by the 1960s the group was marginal to Mexican American politics; if it were not for the steady stream of outside support, the group might have dissolved altogether. In the early 1970s, the organization reached out to the private sector and soon counted such corporations as the Coors Brewing Company, Sears and Roebuck, and EXXON as major financial contributors. LULAC's search for outside monies may be seen as a response to an unstable membership base and a new stage in the group's development. The effort to find reliable sources of income was a reaction to the decline in membership support of a renewed activist agenda. By the 1980s, LULAC political and civil rights activities conducted by rank-and-file members were no longer a prominent part of the group's agenda. As the LULAC leadership labored to secure outside funds for their projects, other political entities such as the Mexican American Legal Defense and Educational Fund, the National Council of La Raza, and the Industrial Areas Foundation rose to the forefront of Mexican American politics.

This strategy employed by LULAC leaders of relying on outside sources of money rather than trying to rebuild an active membership base is the key to understanding the organization's continued survival. Purposive and expressive rewards have failed to inspire high levels of activism, and the group has been unable to provide a set of material benefits. Two factors have prevented the organizational demise of the group. First, solidary rewards play an important role in the group's functioning. Conferences with all their attendant diversions, friendship networks, and LULAC-sponsored dances or festivals provide members with ample solidary benefits. Second, for the rank and file, the costs of participation are quite low. Since the late 1960s and early 1970s, it has been possible to keep the organization alive as professional staff and independently funded entities carry on the day-to-day work of service to the Mexican American community.

The reliance on outside funding has resulted in the central irony of contemporary LULAC activities. A lack of material rewards may weaken membership participation but not result in organizational demise. A dedicated and skillful set of leaders had used the name and institutional framework of the group to secure government and corporate monies which helped make LULAC one of the most well known and active groups in Mexican American politics, yet in 1988 it could claim less than five thousand members nationwide. Because of steady funding from the outside, LULAC is more visible in Mexican American politics than ever while failing as a membership-based organization.

Data and Methods

Data for this research were gathered from scholarly books and articles, LULAC newsletters, interviews with past and present activists, the archives at the Benson Latin American Collection at the University of Texas at Austin, and the LULAC materials collection at the Houston Public Library. Interviews conducted by the author were designed to elicit activists' positions on LULAC goals, tactics, and normative values. Activists were also questioned about specific programs and issues they were involved in and their reasons for participation. Primary and secondary LULAC sources were analyzed for these indicators and how they changed over time.

Chapter Summary

Chapter 2 documents the emergence of LULAC in South Texas in 1929 and outlines the group's attitude toward acculturation and assimilation of the Mexican American people as well as their ideology of race relations and upward mobility. The analysis of LULAC ideology and goals will be structured by the function it served in binding the members to the organization. An account of their activities up to and during World War II will be included.

Chapter 3 chronicles the activist years of LULAC. In the post–

World War II period, LULAC and other organizations like it served as vehicles through which politically conservative activists could press their demand for formal equality. In this period, the organization exhibited all the characteristics of a dynamic volunteer organization. LULAC volunteers were involved in a wide range of activities. For example, they conducted English language and citizenship classes and pressed a number of lawsuits against legal segregation of Mexican American children in Texas schools. Purposive and expressive rewards figured prominently during this time. Their crusade for civil rights went hand in hand with a libertarian ethic and a strident antisocialist stand, one which argued that discrimination provided an opportunity for communist propaganda to divide and weaken the nation.

The group's incentive structure was tailored to an activist membership, and the group was successful at retaining their loyalty. LULAC's mix of ideology and civil rights activism gave its members a means through which they could work for social change. There were ample purposive and expressive rewards for participation: attacking racism, demonstrating patriotism, and achieving equal rights for all Mexican Americans.

The transformation the league underwent in the late 1950s and early 1960s is the focus of Chapter 4. In this period, purposive and expressive rewards were no longer sufficient to maintain membership interest and participation. The bulk of the "Mexican American Generation" who had fought for the achievement of equal civil rights had begun to drop out of the organization. Many believed that LULAC had outlived its usefulness and should change its focus.

Had these individuals continued to constitute the bulk of the organization's membership, this book would be a straightforward analysis of the adjustment made to their demands. However, the group was under pressure to change. The 1960s witnessed the rise of more radical and strident Mexican American organizations that demanded that LULAC become more politically active and press for more radical social change. The ideological and political battle that LULAC engaged in with other Mexican American organizations highlights their understanding of racism, and places LULAC in the proper historical context through which one can understand its subsequent transformation. It was at this point that LULAC's purposive and expressive incentives began to lose their effectiveness. Other platforms and programs began to usurp LULAC's traditional and heretofore unchallenged supremacy in the community. Not only did LULAC members begin to question the need for it to continue as an organization, but other viable political groups offered alternatives for political activists. Thus LULAC began a twenty-year decline as an activist organization.

How the new core of activists revived the activism and dealt with the demands of the more radical groups without increasing the demands on the bulk of the membership is the focus of this chapter. Because the new LULAC activists did not constitute an absolute majority in the group, and members of the old guard could not be persuaded to increase their level of activism, the LULAC leadership chose to seek outside support and funding to increase their political activism. LULAC became heavily involved in government projects and corporate-sponsored programs. In the process, the group became more dependent on this outside support and less dependent on membership participation. The organization survived without providing material benefits for the membership at large and secured continued member loyalty by drastically decreasing its demands on the rank and file. In Chapter 5, a summary analysis of LULAC history will be presented. The contemporary activities of LULAC will also be examined in relation to the theoretical assertions made in Chapter 2.

2. Expressive and Purposive Incentives, 1929–1945

During the second decade of the twentieth century, two events set forces into motion that would alter race relations in South Texas. The first was World War I, which would stimulate the economy and create new job opportunities for Mexican Americans. Second, the Mexican Revolution would create a new flow of Mexican immigrants to the United States. From 1920 to 1929, over 500,000 people emigrated to the United States from Mexico, a number that was bolstered by the continued flow of undocumented immigrants (Reisler 1976). The economic stimulus would aid the social and economic integration of the established Mexican American community while the wave of immigration from Mexico would create new fears among the Anglo American population that a "flood" of immigrants was moving into South Texas. One response to the new situation was exhibited by such political organizations as the Order Sons of America (OSA), which proposed social assimilation into American society as a means of resolving the conflicts between Anglos and Mexican Americans. Established in 1918 and representing the upwardly mobile sector of the Mexican American people, the OSA was a nonpartisan civic organization whose energies were focused on activities such as voter registration drives, citizenship classes, and jury selection (Navarro 1974: 62).

The OSA was a fraternal society made up mostly of professional and white-collar workers, the small but growing Mexican American middle class whose relative affluence set them apart from the rest of the minority population. A successor of a mutual aid society (Liga Mexicanista de Beneficencia y Protección), the OSA sought political power through the ballot box. Its political agenda included the right to serve on juries, use public beaches along the coast of Corpus Christi, and sue Anglo Americans in court (J. Hernández 1983: 73). Many of the OSA's activities were also a response to large-scale Mexican immigration to the United States. There was a fear on the part of these middle-class and white-collar Mexican Americans that South Texas would soon be overwhelmed by the new arrivals and that their own status would be undermined if the Anglo population failed to differentiate them from the working-class immigrants (Barrera 1985: 15).

There was also a conflict between the two groups for employment opportunities. Established Mexican Americans resented the newcomers, who accepted lower salaries and thereby depressed the wages of both groups (J. Chávez 1984: 103). Barrera (1988: Chap. 3) has argued that the establishment of the Order of Sons of America was the first organizational sign of a diverging identity between the more established Mexican American residents and the newer *mexicano* arrivals. The apprehensions of the middle-class natives had been bolstered by the wave of paranoia that swept Texas following the Plan of San Diego raids, the 1920–21 pressures for repatriation of Mexican immigrants, and the rampant nativism of the period. By stressing American citizenship and the mastery of English, the Sons of America sought to reassure Texas Anglos that Mexican Americans could be trusted to be loyal and upstanding citizens. They promoted this image by limiting their membership to U.S. citizens and placed an emphasis on acquiring naturalization papers (Barrera 1988).

Groups such as the OSA tried to ease the fears and concerns of the Anglo-Saxon as well as the established Mexican American community. They would argue that they were "old" American stock and that discrimination against them represented a departure from a long history of amiable race relations. They also identified the source of their problems as the recent immigrants, people who threatened descendants of the earlier settlers because of their great numbers, poverty, and attachment to their Mexican nationalism (J. Chávez 1984: 86). One early LULAC spokesperson tried to differentiate between the two groups by asserting that before the wave of immigration during the 1920s and 1930s "there had never been any differences or distinctions between old Texans of Anglo Saxon descent and old Texans of Latin American descent" (A. Hernández 1938). In general it was felt that the newer arrivals provoked a backlash in the white community and threatened the gains made by the Mexican American middle class. To counteract these trends, these early activists would initiate campaigns to improve their image in the Anglo American community as well as to "encourage our fellow Americans of other racial extractions [to] reduce crime, especially among the lower classes, [and to] respect the law" (M. C. González 1932).

In an attempt to coordinate the activities of other emerging middle-class organizations such as the OSA, early Mexican American leaders sought to merge these different groups into a single organization. In 1926, Ben Garza, Jr., a prominent Mexican American leader in Corpus Christi, Texas, contacted other Mexican American leaders throughout South Texas. Individuals such as Alonso Perales, Louis Wilmont, Joe Garza, Andrés de Luna, Manuel González, James Tafolla, Sr., J. T. Canales, and Eduardo Idar figured prominently in these early meetings. After two years of negotiations leaders of the OSA, the Latin American League, the Sons of America, and the Order Knights of America met in Corpus Christi, Texas, to formalize the merger. The result at Obreros Hall on February 17, 1929, was the creation of a new organization, the League of United Latin American Citizens (E. Garza 1951: 4).

Purposive Incentives

The new organization faced the problem of generating the necessary incentives to induce its members to give their time and energy to the achievement of group goals. As with many new organizations, LULAC began with few material resources, capital, or other advantages that could be passed on to its members. Therefore it needed to turn to other less costly forms of rewards such as policy agendas and ideology, those derived from advocating a cause or political orientation (Cigler 1986). The LULAC leadership devoted much time and space in their printed material to promoting their ideology and utilizing it as an incentive with which to attract activists to the fold. While LULAC's numbers would remain small, they would spend the decade developing this vision, which would serve as a guide for middle-class activists for years to come. The historical documents available, though few in number, reveal an organization alive with energy. From 1929 to 1940, its members would be absorbed in consolidating the group, engaging in political and community activities, and debating the fine points of the group's philosophy.

The amount of time the leaders devoted to developing political ideas in their official publications as well as in their private writings reveals the central role purposive and expressive rewards played in the everyday life of the early LULAC. The group provided many of its members with a sense of identity and purpose, people who saw themselves as crusaders, as soldiers in the battle against injustice. As one early LULAC member exclaimed, "The great march of human progress among the Latin Race has started." The organization has proclaimed its mission to be no less than "to claim that God-given right of self preservation, equal education and to abolish once and for all illegal segregation. To erase all racial hatred. To maintain and foster peace, unity, progress, prosperity all under the mantle of intelligence" (T. Garza 1931). The exalted language, the religious imagery, and the reference to the ideals of American democracy were all part of a new theory of race relations and social change. To become a member of LULAC was framed as more than a struggle for equal civil rights, it made the individual part of a moral crusade. Thus, LULAC gave its members ample opportunity for ideological expression and placed them at the vanguard of social reformist movements for Mexican Americans. In short, the reward structure of the new organization centered almost exclusively on purposive and expressive rewards.

A full understanding of how these ideals motivated individuals to join and participate in the group is only possible if their social as well as economic concerns are taken into account. Gutiérrez (1987: 108, 111) has argued that the LULAC ideological thrust reflected the basic issues of discrimination that faced all Mexican Americans during the 1920s and 1930s and that its program was one of finding the most practical way of dealing with the problem. Early LULAC members saw discrimination as a group issue, and they were motivated by a desire to help their compatriots shed the burden of racism. Nevertheless, LULAC's incentive structure incorporated a specific definition of discrimination as well as a world view that sought to preserve the economic status quo and serve their members' economic interests.

Scholars of the group's early development have observed that LULAC drew many of its members from the upwardly mobile sector of the Mexican American people in South Texas. Dr. Douglas O. Weeks, a professor of political science at the University of Texas who chronicled the formation of the organization, noted that its members came from the upper social and economic strata of the Mexican community. In his words, most members were "small capitalists," business managers, or merchants (Weeks 1929: 12). LULAC also attracted lawyers, doctors, and other professionals who had come to South Texas during the Mexican Revolution or who were members of the elite old Spanish or Mexican families. Many provided goods and services to the Mexican American community and served as intermediaries between the Mexican and Anglo communities (R. García 1978: 54). García's study of Mexican American politics in San Antonio during this period reveals that middle-class Mexican Americans were fully conscious of their class interests when they participated in LULAC (R. García 1978: 42). He argues that the ideas espoused by LULAC were "not the ideas of the working class sector of the Mexican community whose ideology in part was expressed by their unions" (R. García 1978: 56). LULAC saw itself as defending its ethnic group against discrimination, but at the same time it defined a division within the Mexican American community, one based on class and income.

But their social status did not protect LULAC members from discrimination nor did it diminish their concern for all Mexican Americans suffering at the hands of racism. The pervasiveness of racism and violence against Mexican Americans at the time of the group's founding placed LULAC's focus on group-related issues at the forefront of the political agenda. Because of the general hostility directed toward all Mexican Americans, the organization recognized the necessity of dealing with discrimination, the most immediate problem. Thus it proposed a "pragmatic" approach to the race question, one which would bring an end to discrimination and promote social integration. Its constitution and "Aims and Purposes" contained clear statements declaring that LULAC asked for nothing other than equal rights under the Constitution of the United States and an equal opportunity. As stated in the LULAC "Aims and Purposes":

> We believe that education is the foundation for the cultural growth and development of this nation and that we are obligated to protect and promote the education of our people in accordance with the best American principles and standards.
> We accept that it is not only the privilege but also the obligation of every member of this organization to uphold and defend the rights and duties vested in every American Citizen by the letter and the spirit of the law of the land.
> As members of a democratic society, we recognize our civic duties and responsibilities and we propose:
> That, in the interest of the public welfare, we shall seek in every possible way to uphold the rights guaranteed to every individual by our state and national laws and to seek justice and equality of treatment in accordance with the law of the land.
> We shall courageously resist un-American tendencies that deprive citizens of these rights in educational institutions, in economic pursuits, and in social and civil activities. (E. Garza 1951: 20–21)

This pragmatic approach to race relations was a formula to a specific end. LULAC members saw their pragmatism as one which preserved the foundations of the economic status quo and fine-tuned American social institutions to accommodate yet another immigrant group. Thus one finds LULAC activists declaring themselves ready to fight such social evils as the "spread of communistic propaganda that is so destructive to the basic principles of Democracy and of American ideals" (M.C. González 1932). These themes were common throughout the decade as they exclaimed that LULAC would "accept no theory, . . . adhere to no doctrine, . . . follow no ideology which does not carry the star spangled symbol as its standard" (E. Salinas 1939). However, it was their social status that helped shape their ideology and prescribed equally ideological solutions to the problem of racism. Because of their privileged yet precarious position, LULAC's membership had a stake in reforming rather than remaking American society. As a consequence they would be found proclaiming loyalty to the United States and its government even at a time when racism against Mexican Americans was rampant.

Their exaggerated patriotism was, in part, a response to the worsening race relations in the Southwest. Montejano (1987: Chaps. 7, 8) has documented increasing conflicts between Mexican Americans and Anglo Americans in Texas at the time and the trend toward segregation, especially in rural areas. By the beginning of the Great Depression, many communities throughout the Southwest and Midwest had organized campaigns to repatriate Mexican nationals. Over 500,000 Mexicans, half of whom were born in the United States and thus were U.S. citizens, were forced to relocate in Mexico (Hoffman 1979: Chap. 7). The 1930s was also a decade in which the middle class felt pressured by the strike activities of the Mexican working class throughout the Southwest (R. García 1983). The Mexican American working class in Texas initiated a surge of unionism and strike activities in agriculture throughout the 1930s. Likewise, workers in the railroads, mines, and other industries exhibited unrest at the onset of the Great Depression (Barrera 1979: 109–110).

Events of the 1930s pitted LULAC's ethnic loyalty against its economic interests and aspirations. On the one hand, LULAC ideologists recognized that discrimination empowered the Anglo and perpetuated Mexican American subordination. On the other hand, they did not believe that the economic system trapped individuals within certain strata nor that the unequal distribution of wealth was in itself unfair. The concern was with discrimination, a phenomenon the group believed it could abolish, and with what they believed was the Mexican American people's special responsibility to demonstrate that racist stereotypes were unfounded. These feats would be accomplished by publicly challenging racist ideas and practices and through cultural assimilation. At the same time, the Mexican American community must adapt itself to American society and prove through behavior, customs, and attitudes that they were worthy of becoming part of American society.

LULAC recognized that poverty was the major social problem which plagued the Mexican American community and that much of it was due to discrimination. Racism had trapped many of its people within the ranks of the working class, but LULAC believed that American society was fluid enough to accommodate the Mexican-origin population given the right combination of political and social activism. The overall campaign against racism was couched within the framework of fulfilling the "obligations" of American citizenship before asserting citizenship's legal rights and protections. LULAC engaged in high-sounding rhetoric as it embraced the notion of complete loyalty to the United States and an intricate system of Americanism (Sandoval 1979: 13; Canales 1937: 34). Its struggle for civil rights was a struggle for an equal start in the economic race of life. In the end, it would be the individual, not the group, who would realize the economic benefits of equal rights in American society.

What LULAC did not do was critique social stratification itself. At a time when the country was experiencing an extended economic depression and the free market system was under attack, LULAC remained silent on the question of inequities created by industrial capitalism. Conspicuously absent from its philosophy was a critique of the unequal distribution of wealth or even a call for any aggressive political participation based on race or ethnicity (Cuellar 1973: 564). Racism was the most immediate but not the most fundamental problem facing Mexican Americans. Group inequality had its roots in the denial of an opportunity for the individual; LULAC's struggles were designed to create a context within which the *individual* could achieve mobility, not transform social institutions.

Trying to reconcile these values and goals with the realities of race relations at the time pulled the group in three different and often contradictory directions. First, LULAC clearly was an interest group whose purpose was to combat discrimination. This goal could be accomplished only through collective efforts (San Miguel 1987: 70). Second, it had to deal with an extremely harsh social atmosphere that viewed political organizing on the part of Mexican Americans with suspicion and hostility. To deal with this problem, the group explicitly rejected such conventional activities as participation in electoral politics, bloc voting, or the formation of an ethnic political machine. As an added precaution, public officials were prohibited from holding membership in the league (LULAC 1939). LULAC's activities were designed to bring about equal rights, opportunities, and privileges, the conditions under which individual choice could reign supreme. Under Article II of the LULAC constitution the twelfth statement of its aims and purposes stipulated that they would participate in local, national, and state elections, but only "as citizens and not as a political club" (LULAC 1939). These restrictions, it was hoped, would demonstrate to the majority population that LULAC would not engage in the trafficking of votes, "disloyalty to their country," or any other strictly partisan matter (Girón 1933).

Finally, the group had a conservative vision of social life it wished to promote. Ultimately political decision making and participation were properly an individual affair; ethnic and racial concerns should be secondary to this principle. At most the league's purpose was to prepare individual Mexican Americans to participate in electoral politics and community affairs, but only as individuals. From this perspective LULAC was not an interest group for Mexican Americans; rather, it was "something bigger and more sacred" whose purpose would be better served by "preparing and equipping our citizens to rightfully and democratically discharge our suffrage duties *individually* to our best interests, and those of our country" (Valencia 1932).

Group concerns were forced to the forefront of the political agenda as LULAC had to contend with racist ideas that categorized all Mexican Americans as inferior. Many of the charges leveled against Mexican Americans in those times revolved around the claim that they not only were inferior, but also that they were properly and naturally citizens of Mexico. When nativist sentiments fueled movements in the U.S. Congress to restrict immigration from Mexico in 1930, LULAC immediately published a rebuttal which harshly criticized the claim that Mexicans "were of an inferior race, of a degraded nature and incapable as well as unworthy of being assimilated into the American civilization" (A. Perales 1930). Over and over again, LULAC asserted that its cultural heritage was something to be proud of. The LULAC code called upon the Mexican American to "be proud of your race and maintain it immaculate, respect your glorious past, and help to defend the rights of your people" ("LULAC Code," 1940).

LULAC went to great lengths to assert that the Mexican culture was ennobling and that their membership's abilities and potentials were equal to those of the Anglo-Saxon. But in the final analysis, Mexican culture was part of their glorious *past*, an aspect of their lives that they should be prepared to compromise on in the interest of social mobility. To this end, LULAC devised a strategy that called for the dissolution of cultural and social boundaries between Anglos and Mexican Americans. At the very least Mexican Americans should adopt a bicultural life-style. The LULAC code called upon members to study their cultural heritage and be proud of it but to also adopt the culture and mores of the United States, "the country to which you owe your allegiance." Members were urged to "learn how to master the two most essential languages—English and Spanish" ("LULAC Code," 1940). As one LULAC member argued, "We must teach our children that every time they are using the word 'American' in order to designate their fellow citizen, the Anglo-American, in a conspicuous manner, *they are segregating themselves* from the American masses of the United States" (Naranjo 1937). Others suggested that parents must assume responsibility for breaking down cultural barriers and "teach the younger generation to strive to be first in everything that is undertaken; but . . . not encourage racial competition. It is the seed of ill feelings." Others believed that a complete assimilation into the American social mainstream must be accomplished and that Mexican Americans should "encourage the conglomeration and blending of races at the expense of distinction. Do as the Gringos do if at all possible. Talk the English language in your homes" (Alvarado 1934).

No other issue generated more controversy within the Mexican American community than LULAC's stand on the issue of Mexican culture and identity. It was attacked by the more traditional *mutualistas* (mutual aid societies) and other members of the community who held fast to their Mexican culture and identity. For some LULAC members, the debate even reached a personal level. One activist and past national president reflected on his early participation in LULAC and recalled that "my own relatives were ridiculing me for being in LULAC" (Herrera 1985). LULAC members were quick to point to their pride in their cultural heritage but to remind their critics that to live in the United States implied an obligation to absorb the customs and mores of the dominant culture. Very early on, the question of national and cultural identity was posed in a clearcut manner as one member queried: "Simply because we are of Mexican descent, does that mean that we have two countries?" (de Luna n.d.a).

LULAC declared that all Mexican Americans should give up any notion of ever returning to Mexico or creating separate ethnic enclaves in the United States. Alonso Perales argued that those individuals who did not recognize the basic differences between the two peoples were not facing up to reality. They were distinct social entities subject to different influences and embarking on different paths of development (A. Perales 1929b). Others voiced the opinion that Mexican citizens residing in the United States or Mexican Americans who still proclaimed allegiance to Mexico should live in Mexico. LULAC reminded both the Anglo and Mexican American community that Mexican-origin people shaped the course of American history and that many Mexicans fought against Mexico in the war for Texas independence. John J. Rodríguez, an early LULAC member, prided himself on his North American heritage when he asserted that "my father was eighth generation and I am a ninth generation Texan" (Herrera 1985). Another put it this way: "We are called renegades and anti Mexican [by those still loyal to Mexico], we call them visitors" (Taylor 1934: 316).

The line between the two peoples and cultures would become a point of contention within the organization when LULAC's leadership attempted to explain the gap between potential and actual achievement in the Mexican American community. If one is reluctant to offer structural arguments to explain the subordinate position of the Mexican American, a way to do it without admitting inferiority had to be found. One solution was for LULAC leaders to employ historical explanations to account for its own people's lack of achievement. Some LULAC ideologists argued that the problem was primarily that of the immigrants and traced their problems to their recent experience in Mexico. Implying that it was only a matter of time before the Mexican American adapted to North American society, one early activist noted that these unfortunate individuals were a "product of . . . cruel masters who held them under the bondage of ignorance" (Ruiz 1932a). Others held that Mexican Americans could be favorably compared to a natural resource, albeit one in need of extensive refinement:

> [The Texas-Mexican] is a part of Mother Earth, it has in its bosom, deep down in its heart, precious metals, gold, silver, diamond, oil, in fact, precious friendship, golden deeds, diamond-spirited citizens, but those things are not apparent on the surface as yet . . . In seeking for the treasure we will encounter hard strata of solid rock . . . The reward for our labor is not to be expected within the first few hundred feet of drilling into the heart of men, but after we have spent much labor, thought, energy, time, money. (M. C. González 1930)

These were relatively benign contentions if one accepted the argument that the individual was largely responsible for his or her lot in life. Others were not so charitable and reached more strident conclusions. If Mexico and Mexican culture were associated with poverty and ignorance, separating Mexican culture from the social condition of the Mexican sometimes became problematic. LULAC's focus on individual initiative left some members with the fear that Mexican Americans themselves might possess some inherent flaws. Indeed, early LULAC statements revealed a tendency to stereotype its people's abilities in much the same way the Anglo-Saxon did. If the walls of discrimination were crumbling and opportunities abounded for the industrious, why the gap between potential and achievement? One alternative is to place the onus of failure on the Mexican people themselves. In a moment of indiscretion, Alonso Perales, a principal founder of LULAC, lamented what he regarded as the fact that Mexican Americans were a docile people content with their "primitive lives" (A. Perales 1931: 4). In a letter to Ben Garza, he confided that

> although I am an American citizen and the United States is the leading
> country in the world, I belong to the Mexican-American component ele-
> ment of our nation, and as a racial entity we Mexican-Americans have
> accomplished nothing that we can point to with pride. Now, then, the
> question is: Are we going to continue in our backward state of the past,
> or are we going to get out of the rut, forge ahead and keep abreast of
> the hard driving Anglo-Saxon? There is the big problem before us, my
> friend, and one that we Mexican-Americans must solve if we have
> any sense of pride at all. (A. Perales 1928)

Even the simple task of political organizing seemed lost on these contentious and unenlightened people from the point of view of some early organizers. As James Tafolla observed:

> I know how hard it is for our people to get together and I think I called
> special attention to this fact when I spoke before the Harlingen Conven-
> tion and told the story about the Greeks, the Chinamen and the Mexi-
> cans—the first two races always getting together and establishing some
> sort of profitable business and the Mexicans always getting together and
> establishing a real, sure enough fight. If you can eradicate this charac-
> teristic from our race, you are welcome to it, as I have given it up as a
> hopeless task. (Tafolla 1927)

These disparaging remarks were exceptions to the dominant thrust and development of LULAC thought. The genius of LULAC's purposive and expressive incentives was the promise of improved race relations and greater economic mobility, simultaneously with preserving the foundations of the society. The demands came from a group of reformers who believed the American free enterprise system was normatively acceptable and that Anglos would eventually accept Mexican Americans as their social equal. To bolster their arguments, they would point to examples of Mexican Americans who had achieved a degree of success. Many of these people were LULAC members, the best and the brightest of their race, examples of the inroads Mexican Americans could make into Anglo American society (E. Salinas 1937: 7). Political reform was important, but individual merit and industry would be the ultimate test of a person's worth. There was no doubt in their minds that through "upbuilding" Mexican Americans could eventually assimilate into the American melting pot (Canamar 1931).

But this process of assimilation was not one which would occur in and of itself, and the responsibility for social mobility was ultimately the individual's. The effects of racism and poverty would emerge as relatively minor impediments to the success of a talented and determined individual. Even at the height of the Great Depression, LULAC activists refrained from criticizing private enterprise or calling for expanded public assistance programs. Whenever these matters were discussed, they were seen as programs established only as temporary emergency relief measures, and the membership was warned about straying too far from individual self-reliance. Noting an apparent lack of motivation on the part of some Mexican Americans one LULAC member remarked,

> Is it that we have instinctively become so dependent that we are left dumbfounded with no initiative whatsoever? The loss or failure to develop a sense of initiative or independence is the greatest catastrophe that can befall an individual. One who hasn't this sense does not live but merely leads a robot existence doing what he is told and being unable to solve his own problems . . . If we are suffering from "dependicitis" let us perform a major operation at once. Let us rid ourselves of a great drawback for the prognosis of this "disease" is always fatal. (N. Martínez 1940)

From LULAC's perspective, it would behoove the Mexican American to follow the example of the Anglo-Saxon. Alonso Perales claimed that "our Saxon fellow-citizens have, among many others, the great virtue of knowing how to lose a good fight with the same calm and resignation that characterizes them when they conquer in a debate, wager, or whatever it be. The Saxon smiles and congratulates the victorious adversary in place of becoming disgusted and taking vengeful measures unworthy of noble and sincere men" (A. Perales 1929a). In another context, he went on to say that the solution to the problem of discrimination could be taken care of through the democratic process. Mexican Americans would have to take direct responsibility for their own future. Indeed, if Mexican

Americans are suffering at the hands of prejudiced governing officials, he believed that "we have no one to blame but ourselves"
(A. Perales 1929d: Part 5).

Purposive Benefits and Political Action

The LULAC political platform was a call to action, a demand made
upon the membership's time and energy. The record reveals that
many individuals heeded the call. The organization experienced
rapid growth in the ten years before the Second World War, albeit on
a small scale, and in November 1929, Ben Garza reported that there
were nineteen active councils in South Texas (Garza 1929). By 1932,
thirty-seven LULAC councils throughout South Texas were dedicat-
ing their time to building the organization and to pursuing a long
list of political objectives.

Given the problems that Mexican Americans faced in South
Texas, achieving equal civil rights would require massive change,
and some leaders of the organization defined the group's mission in
a way that placed a heavy burden of participation on its members.
Alonso S. Perales asserted that a good council was one that attended
to such matters as education, health, social hygiene, housing concerns, the poll tax, juvenile delinquency, low wages, and home beau-
tification. He specified that only those councils actively engaged in
performing these duties and obligations were carrying out the aims
and purpose of the league and deserved to be considered a "good
council" (A. Perales 1978). Throughout the 1930s the organization
would engage in such activities as voter registration drives, public
relations campaigns, letter-writing campaigns, lobbying efforts, and
legal pressure (E. Garza 1951: Chap. 4; San Miguel 1987: Chap. 3).

LULAC's ideological vision captured the imagination of the upwardly mobile sector of the Mexican American people. The energy
and dedication of these early activists who were willing to invest
in the promotion of their ideals were demonstrated by the record
they established in the early years of the group's organizing drives.
LULAC members were assigned the task of traveling through Texas
towns and contacting local officials and other interested parties
in order to charter local councils. These installation committees
would engage in marathon treks throughout the state which came
to be known as the LULAC Flying Squadron. One such trip in early
1932 recorded in the *LULAC News* proudly announced that "Dilley,
Harlingen, Mercedes, Donna and Benavides fall in line and join the
Lulac Banner." Details of the organizing drive documented a long
and arduous campaign that began at 8:30 on a Saturday night and

ended late Monday afternoon. President General M. C. González and nine other LULAC officials visited five separate communities in South Texas and installed five new councils before returning home to San Antonio (Valencia 1932: 4–5).

After that particular trip, LULAC activists felt that they were part of a movement spreading among the Mexican American population (Valencia 1932: 7). The group's ideals and political goals motivated and immersed the individual in a series of activities. LULAC councils would become involved in voting registration drives, the renovation of Mexican elementary schools, petitions, public relations campaigns, and legal pressure against employers or local governments who discriminated against Mexican Americans (E. Garza 1951: Chap. 4).

Another major thrust of LULAC activities before World War II was education. LULAC concentrated on a wide range of educational activities such as back-to-school campaigns (for children as well as adults), citizenship training, and homemaking classes for wives and mothers. LULAC monthly meetings were tools through which knowledge of parliamentary procedure and public speaking would be passed on to the membership (Sandoval 1979: 31). In the minds of LULAC leaders, one of the principal functions of the public schools was to socialize the individual. As one prominent member declared, "Up to the present time, the public school in the United States has been the true melting pot of this great nation, where dissimilar elements of our population, regardless of race or creed, have fused into one people" (de Luna n.d.a).

For LULAC, the key to Mexican American advancement was to reform the American educational system and make it accessible to Mexican American people. These activists would campaign against segregation and the mistreatment of Mexican American children in the public schools and seek to establish a scholarship program for talented students who wished to receive a college education. It was once suggested that LULAC itself establish schools that would teach Mexican Americans English, knowledge of the U.S. Constitution, the Constitution of Texas, and the history and government of the United States (A. Perales 1929c).

Segregated schools, inferior equipment, and the lack of qualified teachers were seen as the primary obstacles to the full economic and social assimilation of the Mexican American (Cisneros 1940). Once these barriers were removed, advancements in educational achievement "would in one or two generations place us . . . and our posterity, on a standard of living equal to and on a par with the most

advanced groups which come to form our American Citizenship"
(E. Salinas ca. 1930). The question of group parity was at the center
of LULAC's battle for educational reform. It demanded that the
schools cease their discriminatory practices and give all Mexican
American children equal access to the public schools.

It should be noted, however, that this demand for equal access was
not a challenge to unequal results in educational attainment or economic gain. Nor was it, in the final analysis, a critique of a stratification system that perpetuated an impoverished life for most Mexican Americans. In a reformed society, only merit and ability would
determine an individual's economic advancement. LULAC's was a
doctrine of self-reliance, and it shunned any implication it was seeking special concessions or favoritism for its people (San Miguel
1983: 347). It fully expected mobility to occur for Mexican Americans as a group, but group mobility to LULAC was more a statistical
artifact than a coordinated movement out of poverty. Once discriminatory barriers were removed, educational and income rates for all
Mexican-origin people would rise as a result of individuals finding
their place in the social and economic hierarchy. LULAC's leaders
were very much aware of the fact that having a society free of discrimination does not preclude the existence of poverty. The market
would eventually reward honesty and hard work, but it would also
punish individuals without those attributes (J. Hernández 1932).

Immigration from Mexico during the 1920s and 1930s created
new tensions between Mexican Americans and the Anglo majority
that LULAC felt compelled to address. This flow of immigrants exacerbated the problem of racial discrimination and intergroup hos-
tilities. Gutiérrez (1987: 64–65) argues that two distinct and polar-
ized points of view began to form on the question of immigration in
the Mexican American community. The first was one which tended
to empathize with the plight of the immigrants. Working-class and
grassroots organizations such as the *mutualistas* and labor unions
perceived strong historical and social ties to Mexico and their common experience of racial discrimination and economic exploitation.

The position adopted by LULAC was one that disapproved of the
increasing number of Mexican immigrants. LULAC members understood that they were identified with these recent immigrants and
the social stigma the immigrants brought with them. One of the
early LULAC activists remembered that "at that time we didn't
want to say we were Mexican-American, not because we were
ashamed—but we wanted to get away from the Mexican because
everywhere you could see signs saying: 'No Mexicans Allowed.' "

Another remarked, "I love my Mexican descent. I love it. But when they separate us they [the Anglos] are looking at us as second class Americans" (Sandoval 1979: 28). Others echoed these sentiments and noted, "The native born don't get a chance. We have American ways and think like Americans. [But] to the average American we are just Mexicans" (Taylor 1934: 315).

LULAC lamented the fact that thousands of uneducated Mexicans were crossing the border, thereby exacerbating already tense race relations. As Mexican immigrants worsened cramped housing conditions, competed for jobs, and became more evident in everyday life, fear and suspicion increased among the Anglo population. The feeling among the white population that Mexicans represented an alien and dangerous threat to American culture and society had a profound impact on LULAC's political strategy. LULAC recognized that racism was so pervasive in southwestern society that the hostility and possibly the violence directed at poor immigrants could spill over and impact the lives of assimilated upper-income Mexican Americans.

Thus, LULAC believed it made political sense to try and disassociate its members from the stigma of Mexico and Mexican society. It was argued that the problems of the Mexican and those of the Mexican American were distinct and, from a practical standpoint, mutually exclusive (see R. García 1983). It was also a way of asserting loyalty to the United States and promoting a strategy of economic and social integration. Indeed, many felt that it was politically prudent to make a virtue of the process of the Mexican American's social assimilation. As one activist recalled: "[We] were undergoing a socialization process in a nation whose culture was so potent that ethnic nationalism and integrity were greatly eroded. This resulted in a desire to accommodate to the United States" (Rosales 1983: 4). Since the process of Americanization could not be avoided, those that had gone through the process should be spared the wrath of Anglo hatred. In the short term, the league concluded that one way to protect second- and third-generation Mexican Americans was to draw a line between itself and Mexican nationals.

The distinction made between its members, the established Mexican American community, and Mexican nationals was but one in a series of critical decisions LULAC made when mapping out a political strategy. In the process of defining its loyalties and commitments, LULAC became entangled in a long public battle over the proper racial classification of Mexican Americans and how they fit into the existing system of racism and social exclusion. In those early years LULAC separated the civil rights battles of Mexican nationals and blacks from those of the extant Mexican-origin population. Establishing a tradition of avoiding an association with black politics, LULAC maintained that Mexican Americans were white and therefore had privileges coming to them such as admission to white schools and public places (de Leon 1989: 164–165). Mario García (1984b: 189) notes that LULAC's claim to a common racial heritage with the Anglo-Saxon was also a part of the conservative Mexican elite's claim to racial and cultural superiority. He argues that "part of their 'cultural baggage' [was] the Porfirian homage to white supremacy."

LULAC's working assumption was that discrimination was stronger against blacks than against other racial groups. Not only was the social situation of blacks considered more oppressive than that of the Mexican American, allying with them in a combined assault against racism would be futile and counterproductive. In the end, the organization concluded that Mexican Americans would be better off if they fought the battle for equal civil rights alone (Herrera 1985). Nevertheless, the politics of race took on another dimension when an organization like LULAC would claim that Mexican Americans, like the Anglo-Saxon, were a white-skinned people. Early LULAC members decried society's tendency to differentiate between "white" people and "Mexicans." They reminded American society that in their veins ran the blood of "adventurous Castelian noblemen, the whitest blood in the world, and the blood of the cultured Aztecs and the fierce Apaches, the reddest blood in the world" (de la Garza 1932). Others not wishing to mince words argued that

there has been a slight misunderstanding between some members of the ANGLO AMERICAN Citizens and the LATIN-AMERICAN Citizens. In this age of Civilization, there is no necessity of a disastrous occurrence. The Great Leaders of the noble men who are very active and anxious to see the United States of America progress in perfect Peace and who are lovers of Democracy, Justice and Humanity are performing an unselfish diplomatic duty of bringing about a perfect understanding between two GREAT PEOPLE, both descending from the White Race. (T. Garza 1932)

The organization also invested considerable energy in fighting the practice of classifying Mexican Americans as anything other than white. In Wharton County, Texas, poll tax receipts given to people of Mexican origin were designated "colored," and LULAC vigorously protested the practice. It was careful not to question the system of racial categories itself but the fact that Mexican Americans were placed in an inferior category. As the organization reasoned,

> If the word "Mexican" has reference to the nationality or citizenship of the taxpayer, it stands to reason that a person not a citizen of this country can not participate in politics in this country. But if the word "Mexican" has reference to race, then discrimination exists and the laws of the State are being violated. It is generally conceded that the word "race" on poll tax receipts is put there to distinguish the black (or colored) and white races. (Treveno 1937)

LULAC even took its battle to the federal government. In 1936, a ruling of the U.S. Bureau of the Census instituted a racial classification system where employers were instructed to classify Mexican Americans in a category designated as "colored" in birth and death records where they had been previously recorded as white (M. García 1984b). LULAC engaged in a series of lobbying activities as soon as it discovered that Mexican Americans would be categorized as part of a group of dark-skinned minorities. The action taken by the Census Bureau was seen as an insult by the LULAC membership, an affront to the dignity of Latin Americans (Rosales 1983: 13). "We are not a yellow race," exclaimed one member, ". . . and we protest being classified as such" (J. Rodríguez 1936). There were political and social advantages to be gained by having Mexican Americans officially recognized as members of the white race. The group was searching for a formula that would give Mexican Americans free access to the economic market even if the basic assumptions of racism went unquestioned. LULAC wanted to make the point that its people were not Asian or Native American. The word "race," one LULAC member argued, was a technical term, through which one could "distinguish the black (or colored) and white races" ("Around the LULAC Shield," 1937).

The attempt to present the Mexican American as being of the white race had its underlying political agenda. In a society where blacks were legally segregated, LULAC sought to avoid those legally sanctioned hardships (Rosales 1983), so the theme of Mexicans as a white-skinned people was pursued with zeal. LULAC members referred to Mexican Americans as "the first white race to inhabit this vast empire of ours" ("Are Texas-Mexicans 'Americans'?," 1932). They argued that the Mexican American was "recognized by law as belonging to the white race" ("Around the LULAC Shield," 1937). In an incident involving a racial classification scheme in the Corpus Christi city directory, LULAC also protested Mexican Americans' nonwhite designation. The directory was designed to differentiate between "American" (Am), "Mexicans" (M), "English-speaking Mexicans" (EM), and "Coloreds" (C). LULAC declared that the system was an attempt to "discriminate between the Mexicans themselves and other members of the white race, when in truth and fact we are not only a part and parcel but as well the sum and substance of the white race" (Mesa 1939). To be classified as a colored person was to invite discrimination, and as one early LULAC member stated, "Nothing said we had to be segregated. [There was] nothing on the books. Jim Crow did not apply to us" (Vara 1984).

However, there is evidence to suggest that these political attitudes carried over into the social sphere and that these early activists did not wish to be associated with blacks socially or politically. LULAC credited a Dr. T. J. McCamant with bringing the Census Bureau's classification scheme to its attention. Utilizing the language of racism itself, it thanked him for helping LULAC discover the "nigger in the woodpile" ("Editorial," 1937). On one level, the LULAC membership recognized that they were members of a dark (rather darker) skinned ethnic group. But to be associated with blacks or any other dark race was considered "an insult" (de Luna n.d.b). Although early LULAC documents often referred to Mexican Americans as a "dark" or "colored" minority group, this recognition did not carry over into its cultural practices. In fact, its members often shared many of the social attitudes of the Anglo-Saxon. One LULAC official related an incident in which he stated,

Recently a group of Negro musicians in this city have capitalized on the unsuspecting good-nature of our people, who employed them to play at some public dances, with the result that this contact has led to a few cases of illicit relations between these Negroes and certain ignorant and ill-informed Mexican girls.

These musicians are now in Corpus Christi playing at Mexican dances, and no doubt will ply their nefarious trade on young girls of our race. Mr. Guerrero will acquaint you with the situation more in detail, and will explain to you what can be done to correct it. Please give him your full co-operation and let us tell these Negroes that we are not going to permit our manhood and womanhood to mingle with them on an equal social basis. (G. Salinas 1936)

Such pronouncements went back as far as the days of the Order Knights of America when American blacks were characterized as too closely related to a backward land (Africa) whose culture (e.g., jazz) was close to that of "savages" (Machado 1928).

The system of racial queueing itself offered a variety of opportunities for those who could successfully negotiate a place in the social hierarchy. Their aversion to having themselves designated as "colored" was based on a realistic assessment of social attitudes and the social consequences it held for those defined as marginal to Anglo American society. Racism was real and in the competition for scarce resources every social advantage counted. Their greatest fear was that they would be "shown less consideration than the Indians or even the Negro" (Ruiz 1932a).

It was a telling sign that the interactive function of race and class was not traced to its structural roots; rather they were seen as problems amenable to a political adjustment. LULAC's analysis of racial discrimination and its effects was insightful, yet nowhere did its rhetoric or prescriptions offer a genuine alternative to the economic disparities imposed by the free market. What LULAC ideologists were expressing was the view that inequalities imposed by racial discrimination were unacceptable while those produced by a free market were an unavoidable by-product of a normatively acceptable economic system.

One consequence of this uncritical stance was an aversion to identify with blacks or other minority groups. Taken in isolation, this avoidance could be seen as a product of both social chauvinism and intergroup rivalries. However, given the ideological sources from which these ideas flowed, LULAC's conservative thrust is evident. In a formulation that revealed a keen understanding of social dynamics, LULAC's strategy recognized that racism in a capitalist economy reinforced social divisions, thus creating a two- (or more) tiered social system (see Reich 1981: Chap. 6; Szymanski 1983: Chap. 10). In a society that judged individuals on the basis of skin color, LULAC sought to avoid the stigma of minority group status.

Solidary and Material Incentives

The early LULAC depended primarily on purposive and expressive incentives to maintain membership interest, but solidary benefits also played a role, albeit a secondary one, in maintaining organizational cohesion. As with other Mexican American organizations, LULAC provided social activities to its members (see Tirado 1970). The new organization held numerous celebrations, dances, and festivals on a regular basis. The first LULAC conference was held May 18–19, 1929, in Corpus Christi, Texas. The two-day affair included a banquet on the roof garden at the Hotel Plaza followed by a formal dance. Three months later, LULAC Council No. 1 sponsored a commemoration of the first anniversary of the drive to unify local middle-class organizations under the LULAC banner.

The festivities included a banquet at the Metropolitan Café, an initiation of new members, a cruise on the ocean liner *Japonica*, and a dance at Obreros Hall.[1]

Richard García (1978) argued that the upper and middle classes of the Mexican community were united socially because they had common political and economic interests. LULAC was their political vanguard that transmitted a political ideology and analysis suiting their needs (R. García 1978: 59–60). LULAC's first decade of existence would indicate that its members did not neglect the social aspect of their lives or the networking that such frequent contact made possible. Throughout the decade that followed, LULAC provided a variety of social activities for its members. The annual LULAC convention featured political speeches and workshops, but also a long list of luncheons, recitals, barbecues, banquets, and dances.[2] However, the primary purpose of the league was understood to be the advancement of the Mexican American people. In 1939, a plan designed to raise money for a scholarship fund was presented to the organization. It was suggested that LULAC could raise money for the fund through sponsoring a festival where admission would be charged. The idea was opposed by some members because it seemed to direct their energies away from their primary purpose. It was argued that LULAC was a "civic and patriotic" group rather than a social club. That attitude prevailed throughout the post–World War I period, and not until 1947 did the idea finally have enough backing from the general membership, and the annual fundraiser, La Feria de las Flores, become a LULAC-sponsored event (Rodríguez 1952).

The more pressing question for this period of LULAC history concerns the material rewards members could expect to garner as a benefit of membership. Earlier in this chapter, it was argued that LULAC's vision suited its members because it offered a political platform with a unique appeal to its middle-class members. LULAC itself had no material rewards to offer its members. There were no jobs, insurance policies, or monetary rewards to be gained through becoming a member of the group. LULAC regularly published the *LULAC News*, the group's official newspaper, but other than this nominal networking was the only perk.

The appeal or role that material incentives could play in the attachment of the group was limited for two reasons. First, the group was relatively new and purposive, and ideological incentives tend to dominate emerging organizations. The novel and developing ideology LULAC put forth was enough to motivate its middle-class constituency to action. The lofty terms with which these individuals described their mission spoke of a group dedicated to a cause. Second, LULAC members had something to gain from participating in the organization: the elimination of discrimination against Mexican Americans and the gain these middle-class and professional individuals could realize through improved race relations. The conceptual and practical problem with this argument is that LULAC offered the promise of material gains in the free market. The prize it offered was the opportunity to compete for material goods outside of the group itself. This did not preclude the possibility of LULAC offering material rewards or that these rewards would assume an increasing importance in the future, but for the reasons cited above, material rewards from LULAC were limited in its first decade of life.

Conclusion

Purposive and expressive incentives dominated the league's early politics, and LULAC members were offered the ideal of equal civil rights for Mexican Americans. A cadre of leaders who sold LULAC's set of incentives to the Mexican American community was quick to form. Responding to the call, prominent Mexican American civic leaders such as Ben Garza, Alonso Perales, M. C. González, Andrés de Luna, J. T. Canales, Joe Garza, and Luis Wilmont became key movers in the new organization. During this time membership increased dramatically. Twenty-five delegates and 125 "observers" attended the founding of LULAC in Harlingen in 1929 (Weeks 1929), and approximately 250 members representing 9 councils from South Texas attended the first LULAC convention in Corpus Christi in 1930. By 1940, the organization claimed 150 councils in Texas, New Mexico, Colorado, and California for an approximate membership of 2,000.[3] The dramatic growth of LULAC membership as well as its expansion into three states within a ten-year period demonstrate the vigor with which the group's ideas and programs inspired Mexican Americans throughout the Southwest. It was also a testament to the willingness of these individuals to sacrifice for the organization. Many gave freely of their time and energies to the newly formed organization. Neither the leadership nor the rank and file received compensation directly from LULAC, but through its dedication to eliminating a system of racial discrimination, the organization provided ample inducement for individuals to contribute time, energy, and leadership.

In a racist society, seeking a collective good made social as well as economic sense to these upwardly mobile Mexican Americans. That is, for these individuals with a long-term stake in Anglo American society, joining LULAC advanced their personal situation. For these individuals, the cost of joining and participating in LULAC was comparatively low, since the cost of not joining was potentially high. In other words, they stood to gain so much from the collective good that they had an incentive to contribute toward its realization (Moe 1981: 534). LULAC membership could derive purposive or expressive rewards by crusading against racism, but their participation would provide material benefits in the long run, although not necessarily through the organization per se. Any material benefit they derived would flow to them as a by-product of LULAC activities.

One potent element in LULAC's incentive structure was the elimination of racism and the promise of future integration. What was demonstrated with its analysis of racism was an ability to integrate discrimination and exclusion into a single political analysis of group conflict. Given its previously stated values, racism would have to be attacked through existing governmental agencies and, more important, "only with the cooperation of the school teachers, the Chamber of Commerce, . . . and the Anglo Saxon citizens in general" (Recio 1932). LULAC's faith in the system was an affirmation of belief in its fairness and LULAC's desire to preserve it intact. In fact, LULAC members would argue that racism was only a temporary aberration perpetrated by a small minority. When the league's members called for equal civil rights for Mexican Americans, they saw themselves as uniting with the great majority of right-minded Americans. After a decade of frustrating struggle, they still spoke of racism as a problem whose days were numbered:

> Sometimes, under the guise of patriotism, selfish or misguided persons raise the cry of hate and intolerance, of prejudice and disrespect. With the Flag in one hand, they rape that Symbol of its most sacred attributes. . . . Largely through ignorance, individuals and groups seek to ostracize or demean fellow citizens for their differences in customs, language, economic status, or cultural background. Enlightenment and tolerance, coupled with firmness in controlling subversive vested interests, is our safeguard. (Sánchez 1940)

However, as we have seen, incentives do not exist in a vacuum but must be tailored to fit a specific audience and their needs. LULAC had contrived a set of inducements that struck a responsive chord in the middle-class Mexican American community. The group formulated a clear vision of ethnic relations in the United States that sounded the charge against racism while catering to economically mobile Mexican Americans. LULAC's call for loyalty to the U.S. government, "100 percent Americanism," and the adoption of the English language was a demonstration that the Mexican American people could assimilate and become loyal and productive citizens of the United States. LULAC firmly subscribed to a doctrine of social change through peaceful institutional means and would go to great lengths to prove its dedication to the preservation of the existing governmental framework and the free market economy. Thus, its members' understanding of racism as well as their preferred mode of combating it were couched within a larger social philosophy. Their vision was of a more just society, one that revolved around individual merit and achievement. Group benefits could be derived through their struggle to eliminate racist restrictions against their people, but a class hierarchy along with its unequal distribution of wealth would remain intact. In the long run, group advancement would be the sum of individual achievement (or failure). As they worked long and hard against the oppressive and omnipresent burden of racism, it was accommodation to the American system that they wanted, not a rearrangement of its foundations.

3. Collective Goals and Individual Mobility, 1945–1960

LULAC survived its first decade (1929–1939) through a reliance on ideological expression and a political agenda as an inducement for political participation. Its political conservatism and incremental approach to social change served to maintain an organization structure and to elicit active participation from its members. Whether the group would have had to rely more heavily upon material or solidary rewards over time, as our model would predict, became a moot point. Patriotic fever during World War II gripped the organization and LULAC members joined the war effort en masse. In the process some of them made great personal and monetary sacrifices when they joined the armed services. Frank J. Galván, Jr. (LULAC president 1936–37) was a lawyer in El Paso who jumped at the chance to fight in the war: "I volunteered into the service. I was not drafted. I didn't wait to be drafted. I was anxious to get into the struggle, precisely because I have a love and affection for my country, my adopted country. I volunteered into the service on March the 3rd, I think, 1941 [sic]. Right after Pearl Harbor, I made arrangements to close the law office, and volunteered. . . . I was impatient and the draft wasn't doing anything, so I closed my office" (Galván 1975).

With the onset of World War II, LULAC fell into a dormant period, and between 1941 and 1945 most LULAC councils became inactive due to lack of membership. Eager to prove their loyalty, the ranks of LULAC were depleted when many of its members volunteered for the armed services. Ben Osuna was elected president general of LULAC in June 1942 and entered Officer Candidate School in August of that same year. The presidents who served until 1945 were little more than caretakers, World War I veterans whose function it was to maintain some semblance of organizational activity ("LULAC through the Years," 1954: 64, 74). It was a time for patriotic Americans to do their part. As George Garza put it, LULAC "gave unreservedly of its manpower to the service of its country" (G. Garza 1954). Active membership fell and, with a few notable exceptions, many of the league's activities ground to a halt.

At the end of World War II, the Mexican American political community experienced a major upheaval, one that would have profound effects on LULAC. The post–World War II period would bring home thousands of Mexican American veterans immersed in the ideals of freedom and equality, two ideals they sought to apply at home (Cuellar 1973). With a booming postwar economy and social services such as the GI Bill providing access to higher education, the tools and materials necessary for the integration of America's minorities were available. The goals of equality and democracy promoted in the conflict by the United States allowed Mexican American leaders to utilize these themes to promote the social and political advancement of their people (Alvarez 1973). These individuals have come to be known as the Mexican American generation, a cohort of Chicanos who grew up in the United States during the Depression and became politically active after World War II. They were idealistic individuals committed to the reforms of the New Deal, the promise of a new political order, and the democratic process. The Mexican American generation had broken completely with the immigrant's focus on Mexican politics and was concerned with such questions as political accommodation and cultural assimilation, the issues of the American citizen (M. García 1984a).

At this time a number of Mexican American political organizations were created. The American GI Forum was established in Corpus Christi, Texas, to help returning veterans obtain governmental benefits. The organization quickly extended its scope of activities to include such issues as school desegregation, undocumented laborers, and political representation (Allsup 1982: 29–38). In Los Angeles the Community Service Organization (CSO) worked on issues such as police brutality, education, and integrated housing (Barrera 1988: 10). Other groups such as the Coordinating Council for Latin American Youth (CCLAY) worked to convince the local power structures of the value of reform. Many of these were distinctly middle-class groups, like CCLAY, who sought integration rather than separation from American society (M. García 1984a: 279–282). For those Mexican Americans with a real or potential stake in society, the opportunity for a better life was at hand.

It was in this context that LULAC began anew. This process involved the re-recruitment of some older members, but for the most part the organization served as a vehicle for younger Mexican American activists, veterans of a conflict that promised political equality and democracy for all people. As far as the organizational development of LULAC was concerned, the post–World War II period was important in two ways. First, it was the time in which membership activism would reach its height. Petitions, community projects, and legal activity were continuing concerns on the LULAC agenda. Even with a lack of material incentives LULAC successfully inspired a high level of member participation and was able to score a number of important victories in the area of civil rights as well as numerous other achievements on the local level. Along with other organizations such as the GI Forum and the CSO, LULAC would be on the cutting edge of the fight against segregation and racial discrimination. It was a time in which the general membership was directly involved in advancing its group goals. In organizational terms, the group began anew and would repeat its first stage of organizational development. LULAC provided an abundance of purposive rewards in the form of social change, personal gratification, and ideological expression. There was little in the way of material rewards, and all positions within the organization were staffed by volunteers. President General Arnulfo Zamora (1945–47), whose job it was to rebuild the struggling organization, summarized the situation in 1945: "This administration offers you nothing but work and more work; sweat and more sweat" ("LULAC through the Years," 1954: 70).

Any material incentives derived through group membership were negligible. LULAC did not even offer such amenities as group health or burial insurance. Solidary incentives in the form of dances, festivals, and camaraderie were the main nonpurposive incentives for joining LULAC. They would assume a more important role in the group's incentive structure as time went on, but at this early stage LULAC demanded that its members dedicate a great deal of time and energy to achieving their political goals. Throughout the last half of the 1940s and the 1950s, LULAC volunteers would pursue educational reform, conduct citizenship and English language classes, and raise money for local charities. They would also conduct campaigns to integrate dance halls, restaurants, swimming pools, and other public facilities (Fraga 1980: 46).

The second important feature of LULAC during the late 1940s and 1950s was that it was a period of theory building, a time when LULAC's purposive and expressive incentives were defined. What it meant to be Mexican American and how that fit into the question of economic mobility was a subject of intense debate among LULAC members in the 1950s. LULAC ideologists wrestled with the question of Mexican ethnicity and the role of the Mexican American in the political economy. This constant discussion of the group's philosophy was an indicator of the extent to which purposive and expressive rewards were to dominate LULAC's agenda and reward structure throughout the late 1940s and 1950s. And like LULAC of the 1930s the group was completely dependent upon volunteer participation by its leadership and members. The key difference between the two time periods was that the group's maturation would not be interrupted by a major event such as the Second World War, and LULAC would eventually fall prey to all the strains and stresses predicted by our economic model of organizational development. These pressures would be further exacerbated as many discriminatory practices against Mexican Americans were abolished. In other words, the drop in member enthusiasm and participation predicted by our economic model of group evolution accelerated as the goals of LULAC were achieved in the 1950s. As major legal battles were won, many group members and leaders began to question the need for LULAC to carry on its activist tradition. Thus the late 1950s would be a period of crisis for LULAC, one where membership and participation would drop and the group would be forced to reexamine its reward structure.

Expressive and Purposive Politics, 1945–1960

The end of the Second World War marked the rebirth of LULAC as hundreds of idealistic Mexican Americans swelled its ranks and breathed new life into its councils. The patriotic themes of the 1930s were adapted to new circumstances as LULAC promoted its vision of integration and economic mobility. Seeking what they believed to be their rightful place in American society, these World War II veterans reaffirmed their commitment to American democracy by seeking peaceful reform. As one member of this cadre editorialized, "We have proved ourselves true and loyal Americans by every trial and test that has confronted us; now give us social, political, and economic equality and the opportunity to practice and enjoy that equality. We ask for it not as a favor, but as a delegated right guaranteed by our Constitution, and as a reward for faithful service" ("Editorial," 1945b). Many of the Mexican American veterans who joined LULAC had a deep-seated belief in the promise of American democracy and the need to preserve its foundations ("Editorial," 1945b). Not only did they feel that racism was cruel and unjust, it was directed against people who were more than willing to prove their loyalty. Fighting bigotry was a way in which all patriotic citizens could remove a blemish on the American record of fairness and justice. As George Garza explained in 1947, he could not understand his being rejected by the Anglo-Saxon: "Why was it that I, who seemed to have been born with an inherent thrilled-feeling when I saw the American Flag; who had learned to love and exalt this country, its history and traditions; and who, by birth, language, training, and practice, considered myself an American, should be looked upon as being different from Robert Baker, Moses Gensberg, and Gerhardt Schule?" (G. Garza 1947).

Individuals attracted to LULAC found an inspiration in its "Aims and Purposes" that moved many of them to dedicate many years of their lives to its cause. The language used by activists at the time and the memories they had of their contributions to the league's projects revealed a set of deeply held beliefs and commitments. One long-time member recalled that all LULAC members took a "vow of poverty" when they committed themselves to working for the group. It was understood that LULAC work would take its toll on one's personal life and that family and career would suffer. The situation was dramatized by one activist who later felt that LULAC's accomplishments were wrought with "nothing but our bare hands, our hopes, our patience and our faith, slow but sure we have accomplished our purpose . . . without millions of dollars given to us by an Eastern foundation, without high-sounding titles coming down to the Southwest to help us" (Herrera 1971).

LULAC harnessed this energy to initiate a fifteen-year battle against discrimination in the Southwest. As in the 1930s, LULAC would reiterate its attachment to American society and its long-standing goal to integrate Mexican Americans into that society. The campaign it waged against discrimination carried also the ideological combination of conformity, patriotism, and free market capitalism. These values were soon put into practice. Not waiting for Anglo society to embrace them, members worked to integrate themselves by engaging in community activities such as the Boy Scouts, the Girl Scouts, 4-H Clubs, Little League baseball, the March of Dimes, and the Red Cross. These were activities that served the community in general, not only the Mexican American people. In the 1950s members' purposive and expressive incentives were defined more globally in order to emphasize their role as participants in the larger society. As one official notes, "LULAC should not be thought of except in bigger terms than a 'minority' organization. This must necessarily be true because Lulac should concern itself not only with minority problems, but overall community problems as well" (E. Chávez 1953). Emphasizing the fact that its members too were American citizens, LULAC showed an enthusiasm for casting aside the ethnic burden. For them, to be a Latin American was "to be given an opportunity to make a great and unique contribution to our State and Nation" (E. Chávez 1953).

One of the first steps they could take toward making a contribution to the nation was emphasize their personal commitment to join the American cultural mainstream. At one point, there was a movement within the organization to drop the term "Latin" from the group's name. They questioned the tendency for "Americans whose origin goes back to Spain, Mexico, or the Central and South American countries . . . [to] assume and popularize a name that will stamp them as a different type of American" ("Editorial," 1947). To speed this process, the league would do all in its power to promote such things as the use of the English language, the adaptation of American customs, and the general education of the Mexican American. M. C. González, a charter member of the organization, once stated that the primary purpose of LULAC was to function as an "Americanization program." It was an organization which would "Americanize aliens and make better citizens of those who are already citizens" (M. C. González 1946).

The ideas which developed in this environment often assumed a religious quality. LULAC's political doctrine emphasized patriotism and complete faith in the American political process and in its ability to absorb the Mexican American. Indeed, LULAC members were called upon to emphasize the positive aspects of their American citizenship at all times. To focus exclusively on the issue of race and racism would be to admit to the white majority that "we considered ourselves separate and apart from the majority of American citizens and had no faith or confidence in our rights of equality of treatment in accordance with the law of the land" (Montalbo 1957). If there were any problems that Latin Americans faced, they should be worked out with "our Anglo friends" (Montalbo 1957).

Given these values, identifying the sources and causes of racism would present the most difficult theoretical and tactical problems for LULAC. The first issue the organization had to reconcile was the contradiction between its members' love of country and that country's pervasive racism. LULAC could not very well proclaim that American society was fundamentally flawed or that its economic system was oppressive. The organization's first decade of political and theoretical work formed the organizational building blocks of the 1950s. LULAC became wedded to a system which valued the American social system above all else. The persecution of progressive and left-wing organizations by Wisconsin Senator Joseph McCarthy only reinforced LULAC's own conservative and patriotic proclivities. LULAC rejected any claim about the inevitability of racial and class conflicts or any other doctrine that presupposed the existence of deep-seated or irreconcilable conflicts within society. However, it would be perfectly acceptable to assert that discrimination was a temporary aberration, remediable at a relatively low social cost. In its political propaganda, the league argued that racism was strictly attitudinal, a series of erroneous ideas perpetuated from generation to generation. Furthermore, these ideas could be corrected through education and persuasion.

Still, there was a harder edge to the objectives and values of the group. LULAC fought vigorously for equal legal rights and economic opportunity for Mexican Americans, but at the same time the group was highly selective in the aspects of American life it wished to change. These members of the Mexican American generation had experienced racism first-hand, yet they believed that American society was making some reforms in its treatment of minorities. These changes captured the imagination of LULAC membership and convinced them that American society was capable of changing for the better.

Their belief in the value of reforming rather than remaking society was reflected in the theoretical connections they made between racism and outside threats to American society. The league did not adopt the notion of an economic structure which perpetuated the subordinate status of Mexican Americans, though it acknowledged the effects that ethnic divisions could have in generating group conflict. For LULAC, racism was an "insidious poison," one which would "pollute the blood-stream of America." Prejudice was more than a psychological illness, it had potentially adverse political consequences. Its patriotic stance not only helped the league avoid the worst effects of the anti-Communist hysteria of the 1950s, it was able to adopt its themes to its own political agenda. Given the presumed Communist threat in the country at the time, LULAC put forth yet another justification for eliminating racism against Mexican Americans. Thus one finds it arguing that racial conflict played upon dangerous cleavages in American society. In other words, "racial prejudice is the opening wedge used in the propaganda of totalitarian [i.e., Communist] countries to divide and conquer. To allow racial prejudice to go unchallenged is to fail in our duty to Our Country" (R. Cortez 1949).

When LULAC began its program of awarding college scholarships in the 1930s, the group required that the recipients of its awards be outstanding students, citizens of the United States, and Christians. When asked why LULAC added the religious requirement, one early member remarked that "at that time Communism was beginning to take root in certain parts of the country. We didn't want [anybody who believed in Communism] because, you know, they're atheists" (Machuca 1975). The real challenge for LULAC would be to call for limited social change in the hope that it would prevent social cleavages from exploding into class and racial warfare.

This strident anti-Communism was not a new element in LULAC thought, but during the 1950s it was given unprecedented force and visibility. From LULAC's perspective, the United States was engaged in a life and death struggle against socialism in which democracy itself was at stake. As one member put it, "LULAC is helping the fight against Communism. Our organization is doing this through community literacy programs, working for elimination of poverty, organizing citizenship classes, curbing juvenile delinquency, helping eliminate the dropout of school problems, equal employment opportunities, and more so by encouraging all programs to educate our people" (R. Rodríguez 1965).

During the 1950s, a large portion of LULAC's world view centered on the struggle between capitalism and Communism, and it saw itself as part of the fight. Sensing that an impoverished, uneducated mass of minorities could pose a threat to society, LULAC worked to facilitate the process of assimilation so that Mexican Americans would be less receptive to Communism's appeals. LULAC's national president, Albert Armendáriz, urged his followers to turn a deaf ear to the false promises of socialism. According to Armendáriz, Communism had been put to the test and failed miserably. His comments are revealing:

> There is nothing that communism can do for the world that democracy isn't already doing better! What does [Communism] deliver? Communism delivers a work-or-starve policy and the dreadful security of a job for life in a slave labor camp. America enjoys a standard of living higher in the worst times than communism gives at its best. Communism delivers elections and ballots with only one name on them . . . prison camps if you vote against the party or even stay away from work . . . so called "homes" of one room for entire families or two or three . . . government dictated wages and prices so fixed that you will never rise above a bare and barren existence . . . riches for a few bureaucrats who keep themselves in power, poverty for everyone else, constant fear, frustration, hopelessness which only death can end. (Armendáriz 1953a)

This position was echoed by others. "Don't let this happen to us," one member exclaimed. "Think seriously about the *freedoms* we enjoy. Behind the Iron Curtain there are *no freedoms"* (Santoscoy 1953).

Capitalism and the competition of the open market characterized the essence of freedom and liberty, two rights that were denied in Communist nations. For LULAC, the ideals of American society stood in contradistinction to Communism's failings. Moreover, LULAC members believed that as capitalism developed, it was realizing the promises of socialism: the common ownership of property and a more equal distribution of wealth. At one point it was even argued that both ownership of the means of production and wealth were being distributed throughout American society. Public ownership of stocks and bonds was referred to as "'Peoples Capitalism', since in America today, the people themselves are the capitalists and the people share the benefits" ("Ford Stock," 1956).

In the members' minds, the work of LULAC lay in uniting the American people and preventing any one group from coming into a violent confrontation with another (Casillas 1953). In peace as in war, "dissention, bigotry, and prejudice hold no place among people whose mutual safety depends upon unity" ("Editorial," 1945a). LULAC realized that racial prejudice did indeed play upon deep-seated social and economic divisions within "free" societies. LULAC recognized the severity of racial prejudice, but what it feared most was the possibility that race and socioeconomic status would overlap to such an extent that the stability of the society it wished to preserve would be endangered.

In this way, the cause of social preservation took precedence over that of race and overcoming racism. LULAC members were extraordinarily hopeful and optimistic about the ability of the Mexican American people to rise above the constraints of discrimination. Throughout LULAC literature, the organization's members celebrated ambition and success in the face of adversity; racism was viewed as an obstacle that could be effectively overcome. LULAC ideologists urged the individual to persevere and become "the greatest success story the world has ever known" (Armendáriz 1953b). George Garza declared prejudice to be something that would test one's mettle, determination, courage, and "faith in the justness that is God's gift to humanity" (G. Garza 1955a). As they would reaffirm again and again, racism was only one of the many challenges that would test the character and abilities of the individual Mexican American.

The claims concerning the individual's ability to succeed in the face of adversity were based on LULAC's confidence in capitalism, American society, and its ability to produce a just social order. LU-

LAC's struggle against racism was conducted in the name of the individual, not the group. With the complete elimination of discrimination, economic mobility would be decided according to the individual's abilities and performance, not through an arbitrary system of racial prejudice. For LULAC members, "equality of opportunity and the right of each individual to be judged on his individual merits are concepts inherent in our American way of life" (*LULAC News* 21, no. 2). Seeking an equal footing or "starting line" with others in society, the league endorsed the free market's system of economic rewards. As its national president tersely stated, "You can be paid in this world only out of what you produce for the world" (Armendáriz 1953a).

LULAC members rejected any suggestion that their people were innately inferior to the Anglo-Saxon and proclaimed an unshakable faith in the potentials of their people and their ability to succeed in American society. Nevertheless, in any given group talent and energy were unequally distributed, and only individuals could translate potential into material success. Even after full civil rights were secured through collective action, economic rewards would not and should not go to those with limited capabilities and ambition, regardless of their race. As one LULAC member observed, "The citadel falls only to him who exerts a ceaseless, relentless, ever increasing drive and holds on till death or victory" (A. González 1954). LULAC ideologists knew that capitalism prescribed penalties for those unable to meet the challenge: "Everyone must rely on his own merits in such a world, and those who find themselves without sufficient strength giving qualities are not safe from discrimination and injustice in it no matter how they are blinded into believing otherwise" (Moreno 1946). The notion that people should receive their share of the economic pie on any other basis than merit was viewed with scorn. As one member exclaimed, "Maybe the day will come when those who excel will not have to be ashamed that they make a few more (taxable) bucks than the dolts who don't. We'd love a world without dolts, where everyone is king, but God planned it otherwise" ("Not the Same," 1957).

These claims further illuminate the basis for LULAC's opposition to socialism or any system that would equalize wages or guarantee job security. As one member argued, "Uniformity is anti-individual, and whatever is anti-individual is an appeal to the masses, collectivism and out of line with liberty loving democracy" ("Editorial," 1953). Likewise, the individual had to be forever diligent to avoid associations that might harm his or her potential: "The man that lives in a free world is able to carve his own position in life according to his abilities and his desire to be either big or small. But a free society has the tendency to create the aggressive and hard working man as well as the lazy and the weak . . . [who chooses] not to advance himself and will drag others down with him in his negative approach and desire to be a nobody" (L. Perales 1961). The demand for equality was based on the premise that each individual should find his or her place in society according to that individual's abilities and effort *alone*. LULAC was not designed as a vehicle through which its members could seek collective benefits or special considerations, nor was it "something behind which its members may hide" ("Editorial," 1953).

The theme of individual responsibility and achievement defined the limits to ethnic solidarity and cooperation for LULAC. Adverse political and social conditions compelled Mexican Americans to work together, but not to reach out to Mexican nationals. LULAC adopted public policy positions which identified recent immigrants from Mexico as having a negative effect on the native-born.

There were two major reasons LULAC felt the two groups had competing interests. First, as Montejano (1987: 229) found, one way racism against Mexicans manifested itself was to identify them not only as inferior but untouchable. In drawing a line between themselves and working-class immigrants from Mexico, LULAC accepted what he calls the "specter of contamination." According to LULAC pronouncements, not only would Mexican Americans have to seek improvement through education and good citizenship, they would also have to work to "decrease our identification as beings foreign to this country to be used only in those jobs others will not have" (Alvarado 1961). Second, the low wages paid by farmowners in the United States prevented many Mexican American families from establishing a foothold in American society and beginning the process of upward mobility for their children. It was claimed that the constant influx of immigrants made the process of integration a perpetual one, and "that a sudden stoppage of this immigration would find us fully and completely integrated within a single generation" (A. Hernández 1954). LULAC argued that competition from both illegal immigrants and contract laborers from Mexico (*braceros*) robbed the Mexican American farmworker of a living wage. As long as the flow of undocumented workers from Mexico continued unabated, the progress of earlier immigrants would stall (Herrera 1954a).

It was argued that undocumented immigrants from Mexico posed a threat to the well-being of all Americans, and LULAC urged that immigration policy be written with that fact in mind. Furthermore, the flow of immigrants from Mexico should somehow be stopped, and those who came to the United States illegally should be deported. One LULAC activist in El Paso recalled that his council was active in reporting undocumented workers to the authorities during the Great Depression: "We did all we could against the illegal aliens, because they were taking jobs away from the native citizens" (Machuca 1975).

There was some opposition within the group when it came to wholesale expulsion of Mexican nationals. The league opposed deportation schemes that would adversely affect the lives of Mexican Americans, aliens married to American citizens, aliens who have U.S.-born children, "law abiding residents," and those with steady employment who could legalize their status. However, during the mid-1950s, when the U.S. Border Patrol initiated Operation Wetback, a program of mass deportation of Mexican nationals, LULAC offered its support. Despite the hardship and disruption the program caused, the league called for support of the program from the Mexican American community. LULAC leaders argued that the program's purpose should be understood "before passing judgment on any report that border patrolmen have used high handed methods in any particular instance, . . . [or] when some of our legal residents and American citizens may be asked to present identification." LULAC urged its membership to be patient, and if any incidents involving American citizens should occur, they "should be carefully analyzed before hasty judgment is passed and harmful criticism is made" ("Wetback," 1954).

Although these middle-class activists would fight for political reform, their conservative political ideology carried with it the seeds of their organization's emergence into the second stage of organizational development as well as its decline as a vital member-based organization. Incentive theory implies that much of an organization's bureaucratization is a function of time and a general weariness on the part of the rank and file. In the case of LULAC, a moderate set of group goals and a considerable degree of success combined to accelerate this process. From the beginning, LULAC's political demands were limited in scope, and most focused on desegregation and formal equality in education and employment. They were reformers who sought to eliminate the most blatant forms of discrimination against Mexican Americans in order that they might have a chance to compete on an equal footing with the Anglo-Saxon in the free market. They sought to eliminate racism so that their people could be judged on their merits and effort. If racism were eliminated, economic mobility would be decided according to the individual's abilities and performances, not through an arbitrary system of racial prejudice. As the group resolved at its 1953 national convention, "equal opportunity and the right of each individual to be judged on his individual merits are inherent in our American Way of life" ("Resolutions," 1953).

Politics and Purposive Benefits in the 1950s

LULAC ideology would guide the group and its members into a number of areas of political activism. At the local level, LULAC councils were involved in a wide range of activities. Christmas toy drives, eyeglass projects, milk funds, food drives, Boy Scout troops, March of Dimes drives, poll tax drives, blood drives, and numerous other charitable or community projects were a regular part of the LULAC agenda during this time period. Fund-raising efforts included barbecues, enchilada dinners, and the ever-present banquet and dance. LULAC engaged in a number of activities designed to aid the Mexican American community, but the primary focus of the organization was on education, the only reform members believed would have a long-term impact and insure the Mexican American's economic advancement. The Feria de las Flores, a fund-raising dance and festival for the LULAC educational scholarship fund, became an annual event sponsored by most LULAC councils. Through the collection of dues and the proceeds of social events, LULAC members had a long history of promoting educational advancement in the community. "We have given 30 to 35 scholarships a year for I do not know how many years," declared charter member Luis Wilmont (Sandoval 1979: 44).

The faith LULAC had in the ability of education to create change was reflected in the energy it invested in educational reform. English language deficiency was seen as one of the key impediments to the success of Mexican American children in school. Under the leadership of national LULAC president Felix Tijerina, a preschool program called the Little School of the 400 began. This precursor of the Headstart Program attempted to give Spanish-speaking children in the United States a working knowledge of four hundred English words before they entered the first grade ("LULAC in Action," 1960). When Felix Tijerina became president of LULAC in 1956, he made contact with several state government officials as well as with officers of the Texas State Teachers Association concerning the problem of English deficiency among Mexican American children. Bringing the results of a year-long study of the problem to its national assembly, the organization authorized the creation of LULAC National

Fund, Inc. Shortly afterward, a Baytown, Texas, teacher prepared a list of four hundred basic English words necessary for children to know in order to complete the first grade successfully. The first class of sixty students was opened in Ganado and Baytown, Texas, and LULAC reports show that only one student of that first class was required to repeat the first grade. Encouraged by the success of the program, the group opened classes in five other school districts the following year (Tijerina 1962).

As with all LULAC efforts, the project was run by volunteers. Jacob Rodríguez served as executive director of the Little School of the 400, and Felix Tijerina was appointed to the State Education Commission to recommend legislation concerning bilingual programs in the public schools. LULAC also paid for most of the program's operation in its first three years. The program became a crusade that demanded personal and financial sacrifice to insure its success. The first summer that the preschool program was in operation, a total of $4,925.33 was spent teaching basic English to 402 children in six schools in South Texas. LULAC bore half of the cost while LULAC's president general, Felix Tijerina, contributed the rest. Without the support of Felix Tijerina, the school program would not have succeeded. In his report to the organization, he observed that he "personally made up the deficiency because it was necessary to find out the actual cost in order to present this program . . . to the Texas Legislature for approval during the coming year" (Tijerina 1958).

The membership was so encouraged by the initial successes of the program that LULAC's Educational Fund, Inc., was organized in 1959 to raise more funds for the project. In 1959, LULAC persuaded the Texas legislature to sponsor the program, and the Texas Education Agency was allocated monies to defray up to 80 percent of the expenses incurred in the program for participating districts. Called the Pre-School Instructional Classes for Non-English Speaking Children, the optional summer program was begun in Texas in the summer of 1960 (J. Rodríguez 1960). From 1960 to 1964 over 92,000 Mexican American children were trained in preschool English through this LULAC-initiated program (J. Rodríguez 1965). Throughout the early years of the Texas Bilingual Education program, LULAC continued to be involved in the project by monitoring the program's progress. Meticulous records were kept of the number of children trained, and local school districts were pressured into accepting the program if there were enough Spanish-speaking families in the area.

It was the dedication and energy that these individuals invested in these educational programs that provided a measure of member involvement in LULAC activities. LULAC's promotion of the state-sponsored program was a statewide campaign designed to bring it to as many Texas schools as possible. With this program, called Operation Little Schools, Felix Tijerina and his followers spearheaded a campaign to get the word out to the Mexican American community. San Miguel has described one of the marathon promotional campaigns:

> On Friday afternoon, April 15, 1960, the Gulf Star was loaded with the promotional material at Houston's Hobby Airport. A host of LULAC members, government officials, and local media persons were there for the event. . . . Departing Houston at 7:00 A.M., the plane flew first to Corpus Christi. After thirty minutes, the flight continued to McAllen, Laredo, and El Paso. San Antonio, the last stop for speeches, was reached at 4:20 P.M. . . . In places where they did not stop, Tijerina dropped leaflets advertising the program. At the scheduled stops, local LULAC members, community people, the media, and in some cases, local officials were on hand to greet the promoters of the preschool instructional program. According to one journalist, leaflets were dropped from the Gulf plane, appeals were broadcast in Spanish over thirty-eight radio stations, television studios ran a documentary film explaining the program, and newspapers headlined the good word. In remote Mexican-American settlements, Boy Scouts carried handbills announcing the opening of the Little Schools. (San Miguel 1987: 155)

LULAC established a record of fighting for educational reform. In 1944, John J. Herrera, district governor of LULAC, led a campaign to force local officials to end the segregation of Mexican American children in Missouri City, a community eighteen miles outside of Houston. Mexican children grades one through five were crammed into a one-room schoolhouse while Anglo American children were taught in a modern school building. After local officials refused to integrate the schools, Herrera and other LULAC officials led an eight-month boycott of the public schools. When the boycott was in progress, Herrera and other LULAC members held informal classes for the children two to three times a week. Ultimately, the local school board agreed to allow Mexican American children into the new school (Sandoval 1979: 36–38).

But school boycotts such as that were rare for LULAC, as the group concentrated its efforts on reforming the schools through the courts. On March 2, 1945, LULAC was party to a suit challenging the practice of school segregation in southern California. In the

case, *Méndez* v. *Westminster School District*, the plaintiffs successfully argued that the policy of segregation violated the individual's
equal protection under the law as guaranteed by the 14th Amend-
ment. The district appealed but the trial court decision was upheld
by the 9th Circuit Court of Appeals (San Miguel 1987: 119). The
Méndez case was used by LULAC to pursue further legal tactics in
Texas. Although the Texas attorney general had issued an opinion
forbidding racial segregation in the schools, the practice continued
against Mexican Americans. South Texas school districts sought
to avoid integration by justifying their practices on "pedagogical"
grounds, that is, alleged educational deficiencies of Mexican American children (San Miguel 1987: 119–120).

In 1948, LULAC filed a desegregation suit aimed at clarifying the
constitutional issues involved in the segregation of Mexican Americans in the public schools. In *Minerva Delgado* v. *Bastrop Independent School District*, the organization charged that, contrary to the
law, school officials in four Texas counties were segregating Mexican American schoolchildren. In its suit, the organization won a per-
manent restriction against segregated classes (San Miguel 1983). In
1953, LULAC pressured the Pecos Independent School District to
end the practice of segregating Mexican American and Anglo children. Although the commissioner of education ruled against the
claims made by the organization, LULAC's crusade against the segregation of Mexican American schoolchildren continued ("Pecos,"
1954: 45–48). Relying strictly on the volunteer labor of LULAC at-
torneys and their staff, from 1950 to 1957, approximately fifteen
suits or complaints were filed against school districts throughout
the Southwest (San Miguel 1983).

The work of the early LULAC was a labor of purposive incentives,
not one of individually consumable rewards. Most LULAC members
had already achieved a degree of education and social status, and few
doubted that American society would readily accept other Mexican
Americans given the proper combination of political pressure and
individual preparation (Pinedo 1985). They expressed the fear that
LULAC would fail in its crusade for educational reform and that
their people would face another cycle of poverty and discrimination.
The failure of Mexican Americans to learn English would "haunt"
Mexican American children throughout their lives, "generally con-
demning them to unskilled or semi-skilled employment and preventing them from becoming citizens in the fullest meaning of that
term" ("LULAC in Action," 1960).

In addition to its legal and political work in the field of education,
LULAC also sponsored several suits in other areas of civil rights. In

Hernandez vs. *The State of Texas* (1953), LULAC lawyers brought suit against the State of Texas before the U.S. Supreme Court and argued against the exclusion of Mexican Americans from jury selection. They appealed the murder conviction of a Mexican American on the basis that in the history of Jackson County, Texas, there had never been a Mexican American called for jury duty even though Mexican Americans constituted 18 percent of the population (Sandoval 1979: 65–66). Over a dozen lawyers volunteered their time and effort for LULAC, as did the legal team of Gus García, Carlos Cadena, and John J. Herrera, who successfully argued the case before the Supreme Court. The nine hundred–dollar sum needed to send the original record of the case to Washington was provided by LULAC councils of San Antonio (Herrera 1954b).

To achieve these goals, they gave of their time, effort, and money. For example, Felix Tijerina did not submit expense accounts to the group for all his activities as national president or for his lobbying efforts for the Little School of the 400 ("Editorial," 1956: 13). In a report to the organization in 1949, George Sánchez reported that LULAC had spent just under $10,000 to fight school segregation in Texas. The newly reorganized LULAC had garnered a substantial amount of money as well as volunteer time toward ending the practice of segregation. It was a process that demanded a great amount of sacrifice and resolve. As Sánchez remarked, "I have spent substantial sums out of my personal funds on this project—money that I could ill afford to spend. I have also given a dismaying amount of my time and energies to this project. However, I have been very happy to make this contribution, for I feel that the elimination of the segregation of 'Mexican' children in this state is an accomplishment worthy of the best that any individual or that any organization has to offer" (Sánchez 1949). He added that clerical and office supply costs were kept low ". . . only because a good bit of the work was done at my office at no cost to the [Special School] Fund." (Sánchez, 1949). Another member, reflecting on the group's projects in other areas, stoically noted that the efforts and expenses incurred by the group were merely "dictates of the League," the obligations of a dedicated LULAC member (N. Martínez, 1940).

Changing Incentives and Rewards

One of the key challenges facing LULAC as an organization during this time was the question of its reward structure. As we noted, LULAC offered nothing in the way of material rewards for its members. The prospect of improved race relations and the material benefits that flowed from it were in the interest of the average LULAC member, but those rewards did not flow directly from the group itself. It was not expected that economic benefits should come from LULAC. As members claimed over and over again, they were fighting for an equal opportunity in the footrace of life, not an advantage or even equality of results. This basic philosophy would exacerbate the problems that the organization experienced with trying to maintain its high level of member enthusiasm and participation. Incentive theory predicts that material rewards must take the place of purposive or expressive rewards if a group is to survive, yet the material rewards generated by LULAC activism were minimal. LULAC tenaciously clung to the notion that the group was strictly a service organization and that to offer material benefits to its membership contradicted that ideal. This would prove to be a crucial decision for LULAC strategists to make. By the mid-1950s the organization began to show signs of losing its grip on the general membership. Luciano Santoscoy reminded the general membership that racism was still strong and the league provided a much-needed organizational defense against these abuses. He framed the question in terms of the rewards members derive from the group and argued that "LULAC is [the Mexican American's] economic and social well being, and we must nourish it as carefully as we would nourish our children" (Santoscoy 1954). Nonetheless, the post–World War II period was one in which many educated and assimilated Mexican Americans were slowly absorbed into the political and economic structure of the Southwest. A Mexican American middle class was being formed, and LULAC members were clearly a part of it. The combination of personal mobility and the lack of material rewards from LULAC took its toll. Santoscoy conceded that the mobility LULAC members were experiencing was having a direct effect on their mobilizing efforts and that "most of us in LULAC enjoy a fairly good standard of living, bringing about our desire to keep up with the Joneses. Many of these Joneses do not like meetings or let it be known that they and we belong to LULAC. . . . Having no time to read LULAC NEWS and attend meetings, little is known of our problems and their solution" (Santoscoy 1954).

Even at a time when the group was fighting some of its most important civil rights battles, a decline in the membership's willingness to give of themselves was beginning to manifest itself. Even the lofty goals and solid dedication expressed during the years immediately after World War II were losing their potency. It had been a decade since the group set out to reform American society, and LULAC's expressive and purposive rewards were losing their punch. This process was not only a function of the passage of time and membership fatigue, but also of those rewards which emphasized equal rights and upward mobility goals, which many LULAC members felt had materialized.

Whether equal rights had actually been achieved in Texas and elsewhere would be irrelevant to the widespread perception among the rank and file that big gains had been made. Largely through their efforts and those of other groups such as the American GI Forum, they had succeeded in eliminating many of the legal forms of discrimination against Mexican Americans. With the victories in such cases as *Delgado* v. *Bastrop Independent School District* (1948), which finally struck down the segregation of Mexican American children in Texas schools, many LULAC members felt that formal equality then became a problem of enforcement. In the mid-1950s, one LULAC council was proud to announce that it had been successful in abolishing discrimination against Mexican Americans and that "today, discrimination does not exist in Fort Stockton" ("LULAC in Action," 1954: 55). Even George Garza observed that LULAC's major battle, the "eradication of discrimination and segregation, is rapidly coming to a close," and that Mexican Americans should now "be prepared to enjoy the fruits of our efforts" (G. Garza 1955b). One prominent member recalled that during the 1950s, the three main objectives LULAC set for itself had been achieved: the mobilization of the Mexican American vote, the desegregation of the public schools, and the elimination of segregation in public facilities (Santoscoy 1985).

There was a general feeling that the doors of opportunity were finally opening up to the Mexican American and that the United States had demonstrated its ability to absorb the latest in a series of minority groups. It was genuinely felt that progress was being made, and as one member declared, "We are entering a new era in LULAC. We are no longer consumed with the thought of discrimination or segregation" ("Editorial," 1956). Comments such as these ran throughout the group's written records, but there were some members who were critical of these innocent declarations. LULAC General President Frank Pinedo (1954–55) frequently criticized those members who were drifting away from active participation in community affairs. Lashing out against the growing complacency of the general membership, Pinedo railed against their self-satisfaction and the declining level of energy the organization could tap for political purposes. He charged that these individuals, "while composed of many shades and varieties, may be labeled for convenience as follows: (1) The satisfied-with-things group, (2) LULAC has-won-its-glories group and (3) The 'Mañana Boys'" (Pinedo 1954).

The debates and concerns of LULAC in the late 1950s reflected these beliefs and the breakdown in consensus over the goals and direction of the group. Slowly, many members began either to leave the group or withdraw their support for additional political activism within the organization. De León (1989: 165) noted that LULAC activity in Houston had fallen off at this time as membership dropped, the Junior LULACs had disbanded, the Rey Feo (fund-raising) project had lapsed, and ceremonies were poorly attended. As early as the mid-1950s, LULAC rank and file began to move away from active participation in the group's political activities and were drawn mainly to its social activities. As Frank Pinedo later recalled, "Too many [of our] resources went into social events. . . . At our national convention, I planned a series of seminars on employment, education, poll taxes, and etc. so members could get informed and enthused. I was disappointed that many of the members spent more time in the hospitality room than in the seminar rooms" (Pinedo 1985).

By 1961, the situation had worsened. Past national president Hector Godínez noted that many of the members seemed satisfied with the political status quo and wanted little to do with increased demands within the group: "In general, however, we had a good number of queen contests, dances, social gatherings, dinners and the usual social activity. It is good to engage in social affairs, since this is one means of raising money as well as of enjoying fellowship, but we should not lose sight of our ideals, our mission, or our aims and purposes" (Godínez 1961). He noted that "a great percentage of our activities this year have been purely social" (Godínez 1961), and that the organization had seemed to reach a "stagnant condition" (Godínez n.d.).

The achievement of formal equality in some key areas of life would constitute the fulfillment of LULAC goals as many of these World War II veterans understood them. The economic success that many LULAC members had experienced contributed to solidary rewards assuming an ever greater role in the group's exchange structure. It is important to note, however, that the greatest structural change in the organization's history would result from its successes rather than its failures. As more and more LULAC members came to believe that the major obstacles to formal, legal equality for Mexican Americans had been eliminated, LULAC exchange formulas had to be renegotiated. The purposive rewards that motivated this group of volunteers were slowly disappearing, and the effect on LULAC activism would be telling. By the end of the 1950s, the league as a whole had begun to focus more and more on local, non-controversial "civic" issues, activities which would benefit not only Mexican Americans but the entire community or nation.

Among the more orthodox liberals in the organization, a reaction to LULAC's past activism had begun to set in as they believed that equal rights for Mexican Americans had been achieved. The original intent of LULAC's political program was to create an environment in which talented and industrious Mexican American people could advance without the fetters of racism. During the late 1950s, the league was criticized by some of its own members for expanding the scope of its educational reforms. Some LULAC members who had joined the organization after World War II opposed the concept of the Little School of the 400 and the system of bilingual education it introduced. In their eyes, these programs implied separation, segregation, and inferiority—phenomena they had dedicated themselves to fight. The shift in values and political strategy that the Little School of the 400 implied to this faction of LULAC caused them to begin withdrawing their active support of the organization. As past national president Albert Armendáriz expressed it, "LULAC's traditional position was that the integration of the public schools in the United States for Hispanics was the key to successful competition with their Anglo American counterpart. Hispanics do not need special classes or special education. Necessity is the mother of invention" (Armendáriz 1985).

Conclusion

LULAC emerged from the post–World War II period as the largest and most influential of all Mexican American political organizations. It was also a durable organization, one that grew and prospered. Its philosophy of patriotism, hard work, and individual merit not only appealed to the educated, upwardly mobile sector of its people, it also challenged them to work within the system for change.

LULAC's ideals and goals pointed to the contradictions inherent in the politics of equal opportunity, but its members were not blind or naïve. When the values they cherished were threatened, the group acted decisively. Throughout the post–World War II period, the organization engaged in a self-conscious effort to divert discontent generated by poverty and racial discrimination into socially approved channels. Ever aware that the impact of racial and class barriers could destabilize American society, LULAC was motivated to eliminate the former. The question of the unequal distribution of goods according to class distinctions was another matter. How the individual would fit into the economic hierarchy was a matter to be determined by the individual's talent, energy, and achievements— factors beyond the scope of group politics.

Large gathering of LULAC members at the founding convention,
May 19, 1929. Ben Garza Collection.

Women's luncheon at the 1951 National LULAC Convention in
Laredo, Texas. Wilmot Collection.

Delegates to the 1948 National LULAC Convention gather for a group photograph in Kingsville, Texas. Maldonado Collection.

Delegates to the 1950 Texas State LULAC Convention in Galveston, Texas. *Left to right, standing:* Felix García, Oscar Laurel, George Garza, John J. Herrera, and unknown; *seated:* unknown, Esquiel Salinas, Juan Solís, unknown, and Luis Wilmot. Wilmot Collection.

R. C. Lozano, president of LULAC Council #1, greets three South
American aviation cadets receiving training at the Naval Air Station
in Corpus Christi, Texas, 1941. Wilmot Collection.

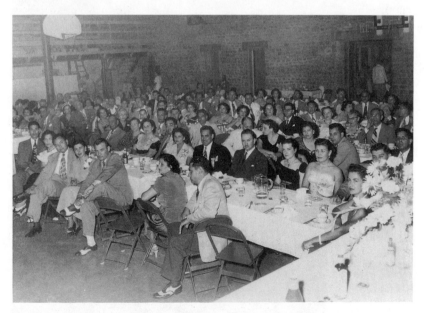

Delegates to the 1951 National LULAC Convention in Laredo, Texas.
Wilmot Collection.

President John F.
Kennedy and Vice-
President Lyndon B.
Johnson meet with
LULAC members at
the Texas State
LULAC Convention
in Houston, Novem-
ber, 1963. Ruben
Bonilla Collection.

President Lyndon B.
Johnson meets with
LULAC National
President William D.
Bonilla, Washington,
D.C., 1964. Ruben
Bonilla Collection.

President Jimmy
Carter meets with
LULAC National
President Edward
Morga at the
White House,
Washington, D.C.,
1978. Morga
Collection.

President Gerald Ford meets with, *from left to right,*
LULAC National President Manuel González and
SER officials Antonio Morales and Ricardo Zazueta,
Washington, D.C., 1975.

Feria de las Flores float, San Antonio, Texas, ca. 1955.
Jake Rodríguez Collection.

El Paso "Rey Feo" 1975. Mike Romo Collection.

4. Mobilization and Transition, 1960–1985

Incentive theory suggests that an organization can mobilize its members on the basis of expressive and purposive interests in its early stages, but in the long run a new set of rewards and a less demanding set of obligations must be devised. In response to a decreased level of activity from the volunteer membership, LULAC shifted its incentive structure from the purposive and expressive benefits offered in the immediate post–World War II period to that of expressive and solidary benefits in the 1960s. The political climate of the 1960s and the availability of federal monies for social programs provided the organization with a unique opportunity to initiate social service programs without increasing the participation demands on the rank-and-file membership. While LULAC appeared to be much more involved in political activity than ever, much of the increased activism was fueled by a new leadership cadre and a new dependence on outside funding sources (see Walker 1983). These activities would mask an evolving exchange relationship between the leadership and followers which centered upon providing an increasing number of social activities in exchange for a modest amount of participation, typically fund-raising and ceremonial activities.

One result of this process was the development of a stable leadership core as the general membership drifted away from political activism. In the late 1950s, a new generation of activists began to join the group in hopes of instigating social change. For the Mexican American middle and professional classes, LULAC was the obvious choice. There were few other political organizations to which they could turn and LULAC was the largest, most visible Mexican American political organization. What distinguished these activists from those of the past and many who were then LULAC's members was the former's desires to address issues that went beyond formal equality. In other words, they sought to set a new course for LULAC politics. As one member expressed it, "Education itself would not do it. Eating might be your priority if you were poor. The limitations [on Mexican Americans] were more economic than anything else" (Robles 1985). From the viewpoint of these new activists, LULAC had ceased to operate as a political entity. One of the new members recalled that LULAC's "credibility was at an all time low. . . . It was a conservative organization for elitist Hispanics. LULAC had to change or become extinct" (R. Bonilla, Jr. 1985).

The ideals and energy that the new wave of activists would bring to the organization would also pose an institutional challenge. In order to redefine the goals of the organization and rekindle the activist spirit in its members, LULAC would either have to convince its present members to become politically active or recruit new members who would be willing to give of their time and effort. Throughout the 1960s LULAC would be surrounded by a sea of political activism and upheaval. The individuals who were attracted to the group during that time would find that the struggle between continued political/economic conservatism and motivating existing members would be the central dilemma facing the group from then on. Incentive theory predicts that renegotiating the exchange in a more demanding direction would be extremely difficult, and by the mid-1960s signs of organizational stress began to appear. It was a politically astute activist who compared its task to a business venture by arguing:

> Are our products good? You bet your boots they are! What about the market? Is there a need for an organization like LULAC? Yes, there is great demand.
> The product is a good one. The demand is great. Why aren't we selling? *The answer is in our members. We need members who are willing to work and make sacrifices*, members who are not content with small gains while there are big, big gaps in the social, political, and educational levels of America's five million plus Mexican-Americans. ("Editorial," 1966; emphasis added)

While it may have been obvious to some LULAC members that an equitable exchange could be devised based on the need to solve the nagging social and economic problems facing the Mexican American community, it was not so obvious to the longtime members. One past president observed that by the mid-1960s LULAC's World War II veterans felt that their job was done and that it was time to withdraw to personal and family concerns (M. González 1986).

LULAC had entered an unstable period in its development. Ever since the first big activist period of the 1950s came to an end, the league had a difficult time maintaining a steady membership, let alone eliciting a high degree of voluntary participation. In 1964, a committee was formed for the purpose of determining exactly how many members LULAC had. The report was telling.

> By actual count, we found that we had 142 councils on the national roster. Of these 98 councils were in good standing with a total membership of 1,990 members. At Convention time, 44 councils were delinquent, dormant or inactive. According to the serial numbers, 400 councils have been granted charters by our organization since its inception and only a little better than a third appeared on the roster of our league and not one fourth were in good standing.
>
> You may gather from this that there is something materially wrong with our expansion program. You may ask, "what has become of the 258 councils that have disappeared from the roster of our league?"
>
> As of November 5, 1964, there are around 2,500 paid up members in our organization. The number fluctuates not only from quarter to quarter but from day to day. (Machuca 1965)

LULAC was in danger of dissolution as its purposive and expressive rewards became a less effective part of the group's exchange structure, and the organization made little effort to redefine the group's mission. The perception that there was less of a need for LULAC to continue as a political entity was but one factor that led to the decline of the Mexican American generation's strength within the organization. Some of the policies that the group had pursued offended many long-time LULAC members before the mid-1960s. What was becoming important in their minds was the need for individuals to take advantage of the opportunities open to Mexican Americans and exploit them as individuals. Ideological arguments that had developed in the 1920s and after World War II were reasserted. The demand for equality was based on the premise that each individual should find his or her place in society according to that individual's abilities and achievements alone.

The Rise of the Chicano Movement

Throughout the 1950s, political organizations like LULAC and the GI Forum enjoyed a predominant position in the Mexican American political community (Allsup 1982; Moore and Pachon 1985). LULAC, the larger and better organized of the two, won the right to speak for the Mexican American people largely by default. However, in his 1968 study of Mexican American political organizations, Charles Chandler noted that by the late 1960s, LULAC as a national organization was no longer a major participant in the Mexican American political community. LULAC had experienced a rapid decline. With the passing of the 1950s other, more radical Chicano organizations began to challenge LULAC's political position and its world view. The aging core of World War II veterans and their newer recruits fought to preserve their vision of Americanism and equal opportunity.

Some LULAC leaders were early critics of the civil rights movement and the tactics its followers employed. The league preferred dialogue and quiet diplomacy over pressure tactics and demonstrations. In 1963, LULAC National President Paul Andow criticized Chicano organizations who pressed for rapid change through confrontational tactics:

> LULAC has been the lone spokesman on Civil Rights for over a quarter of a century. We have not sought solutions to problems by marching to Washington, Sit-in's or picketing or other outward manifestations. We have always gone to the source of the problem and discussed it intelligently in a calm and collected manner. . . . Mass meetings and mass gatherings often times lead to mass hysteria. This paves the way for emotional and irrational thinking which [are] not the criteria for clear thinking Americans. We have been taught to be courteous and highly respectful of all offices in our governmental pattern whether we agree with the individual serving that office or not. (Andow 1963)

LULAC would reiterate its belief that the progress of Mexican Americans came from hard work and from the advantages created by a stable economic and political system. As William Bonilla declared, "The force behind this progress has been and will continue to be a sound education coupled with the recognition and exercise of the privileges of American citizenship" (W. Bonilla 1964b). These changes have come about through "those legal processes guaranteed every American citizen, without transgression into violence, social discord, or civil disorder" (W. Bonilla 1964b).

The league's members were especially troubled by the possibility that such public displays of defiance and impatience for social change could be adopted by Mexican Americans. LULAC decried what it characterized as the aggressiveness and arrogance of the Chicano activists and reaffirmed its dedication to peaceful and orderly change (Salmon 1961). For a generation of Mexican Americans who received their political training in the 1940s and 1950s, LULAC decried the lawless and radical image those groups were projecting to society at large (Avena 1966).

By the late 1960s many new political organizations struggled to correct the desperate social and economic condition of the Mexican American people. What became known as the Chicano movement consisted of a loose coalition of highly ideological and militant organizations such as the Crusade for Justice, the Brown Berets, La Raza Unida party, and student organizations throughout the Southwest. Drawing their inspiration from the passionate rhetoric of leaders such as Rodolfo ("Corky") González, José Angel Gutiérrez, and Reies López Tijerina, they sought to liberate their people from what they characterized as an oppressive system (Hammerbach, Jensen, and Gutiérrez 1985). César Chávez, the charismatic United Farm Workers Union (AFL-CIO) president, made the plight of the impoverished migrant farmworker a symbol of the movement and the problems all Mexican Americans confronted (Kushner 1975). These new organizations represented a threat to LULAC as they absorbed great numbers of community activists, students, and intellectuals impatient with the social and economic condition of their people in the United States (M. García 1989: 11–12).

Although the specific goals of the movement were oftentimes ill-defined and nebulous, the political platforms of the groups involved in its activities were radically different from that of LULAC. As Carlos Muñoz (1987: 42) noted, some common themes included "the quest for a nonwhite identity, and the struggle for political and economic power. The movement attempted to build a 'nation within a nation' through the development of independent Chicano institutions and community control of existing institutions." These groups argued that economic processes and organizations were in need of radical modification and that independent Mexican American political groups were necessary to take the place of political entities such as the Democratic and Republican party machines (Muñoz 1989: 77). These groups also emphasized dignity, self-worth, pride, and a feeling of cultural rebirth as well as the prospect of economic opportunity (Gómez-Quiñones 1978).

A big part of the ideological package individual activists received from participation in the Chicano movement was the sense of group identity and racial solidarity. The term *Chicano* itself was a rejection of assimilation into Anglo American society. The sense of group solidarity was carried one step further as movement activists developed the concept of "Aztlán," the mythic homeland of the Aztecs which was identified as the American Southwest. The term received widespread attention as the myth of the Chicano homeland created a sense of common history and reinforced activists' dedication to redressing past and current wrongs (Anaya and Lomeli 1989). One major appeal that drew activists to the Chicano movement was its unconventional mode of political expression. School walkouts, mass demonstrations, boycotts, strikes, community mobilization, and, in some instances, acts of violence were all activities that drew activists to the ranks of Chicano organizations across the Southwest (Acuña 1988: Chap. 9). The ideology of nationalism and the opportunity to act out those beliefs through concrete political action were an integral part of the incentive package for Mexican American activists who sought rapid and radical social change.

One major charge hurled at LULAC by Chicano activists was that it focused on discrimination only as it would affect its middle-class constituency but showed little concern about political education and the economic welfare of such people as migrant farmworkers (Chandler 1968: 128–129). It was accused of forgetting its people and of being beholden to the government and society. De Leon (1989) documented the attacks that LULAC and other civic organizations in Houston endured when they were characterized as "social clubs" rather than social action entities. These militants argued that "LULAC had forfeited any leadership role in speaking for Chicanismo. Instead of producing men of action, they continued with the old custom of assisting one or two families, offering scholarships of small sums, and hosting fund raising dances, *tamaladas*, and the like" (de León 1989: 177). Criticized by the rising tide of the *movimiento* (movement) for being politically conservative, LULAC fought a decade-long battle with these organizations for leadership within the community.

The public and aggressive stance adopted by Chicano activist groups alarmed LULAC's membership. Their long-stated goals of integration and service were directly challenged by the Chicano movement's cultural and political goals. Many of these new organizations subscribed to ideologies and agendas which challenged dominant institutions, political principles, elected leaders, and organizations within and outside the community (Gómez-Quiñones 1978: 13). LULAC and its middle-class constituency were characterized as complacent and opportunistic individuals aloof from the working-class members of the community. Activists like John J. Herrera and Alfred J. Hernández and others were accused of being beholden to the establishment and perpetuating the plight of the community rather than alleviating it (de León 1989: 176).

LULAC's response to these attacks was to reaffirm its long-stated belief that the country's safety required mutual cooperation and understanding among all racial and ethnic groups. During the 1960s LULAC leaders lashed out against groups they considered to be violent and dangerous. Paul Garza observed that "it stands to reason that we will be called the conservative group by other more militant organizations, but the record indicates that we have done more for our people than all other organizations combined" (P. Garza 1970).

They were also concerned by the increasingly nationalistic and separatist thrust of many Chicano organizations' demands (P. Garza 1970). Many groups were calling for a cultural resurgence among Mexican Americans to counter what they believed to be a loss of their Mexican heritage (see Gómez-Quiñones 1978). LULAC members were incredulous that any Mexican American would advocate the cultural and political separateness they had worked against for so long. It was with no small degree of exasperation when one LULAC activist charged that "no U.S. citizen has ever been asked, much less required to qualify his American nationality by his racial extraction nor descent. Why make ourselves 'Horrible Example No. 1'?" (J. Rodríguez 1970). LULAC members lamented the separatism advocated by Chicano organizations as well as their refusal to accept social assimilation as a necessary and acceptable goal (Flores 1964).

The unrest that LULAC witnessed bore all the signs of unraveling the social fabric it had worked to protect. The theme of Communist subversion playing upon racial strife was revived and, given its rhetoric, the destabilizing effects of class and racial inequality were as much of a threat then as they had been twenty years earlier. During the 1960s, LULAC's concerns centered on the possibility that antidemocratic forces and doctrines would take root in the Mexican American community. One leader noted that the conditions under which Mexican Americans lived in the Southwest were a threat to the American political system. He argued that "inconsistencies, injustices, and discriminations found in the treatment of this minority group, if allowed to continue, may eventually weaken the structure of our democracy" (Montalbo 1966b). Others were more direct:

The greatest of all tragedies, unparalleled in our history is in the making, the duping of many Americans by the communist philosophy that all of the previous wrongs committed by members of our society can be improved or corrected by internal guerilla warfare, property destruction . . . and the annihilation of many American citizens of all races. . . . We have faith that the wrongs of the past can be corrected, that the

American free enterprise system is still the best on the earth, and that truth, "peace with freedom," and good will under God, will prevail. ("The Mexican-American Reply," 1967)

For the league's members, their long-held fears that the problems of racism and poverty were being successfully exploited to drive a wedge between racial minorities and the majority population were coming to pass. Harkening back to their Cold War fears, some argued that a Communist fifth column was marshalling "its minions against established order, organized government, and capitalist systems" (T. Chávez 1961).

As in the 1950s, members of the old guard of LULAC were afraid that the Mexican American people might be receptive to an ideology that they felt was alien to Mexican American culture and history. Some went so far as to argue that because of religious practices, family ties, and traditions, Mexican Americans were the natural enemies of Communism. The successful revolution in Cuba drew the wrath of LULAC. The fact that "Castro's Cuba" was a Latin American nation, and that the people of Cuba spoke Spanish and shared their Latin culture mattered little. For them, "Cuba's leaders today are no longer Latin Americans, they are aliens and enemies" (T. Chávez 1961). As activism among radical Chicano organizations increased, the rhetoric of the LULAC establishment grew more strident and exaggerated. The Mexican American population was spoken of in terms of its unwavering patriotism and its agreement with the doctrines and policies of the state. For example, the war in Vietnam was an example of Communist aggression, an aggression that the Mexican American was proud to counter. One LULAC leader asserted that the Mexican American population had never produced "a traitor to our beloved country in two great world wars, the Korean War or even in Viet Nam where our boys die every day in jungles and rice paddies in a far away land" (Herrera 1966).

Not only did the organization engage in a battle of rhetoric with Chicano organizations, the World War II veterans challenged liberal tendencies within LULAC itself. An example of this internal conflict came during the administration of Alfred J. Hernández (1964–1967), the first president to advocate a more aggressive political role for the organization. An outspoken critic of social injustice in Texas and the neglect of the Mexican American community by President Lyndon Johnson's social programs, Hernández called for increased involvement by LULAC in the broader political and social issues facing its people. He personally participated in the 1966

United Farm Worker's Minimum Wage March, and when the federal Equal Employment Opportunity Commission held a conference that year to address Mexican American employment problems, he led a walkout of all fifty Mexican American representatives in protest of the commission's lack of commitment to change (Rhinehart and Kreneck 1989). The group would demand, and later receive, an audience with the president himself.

This type of high profile political activity was not appreciated by many of the LULAC rank and file. Hernández was assailed for taking unauthorized actions on behalf of the group and for "converting LULAC into a political organization" (Cruz 1969). His critics called on LULAC members to close ranks and avoid public demonstrations and partisan politics. As a spokesman for the opposition argued,

> LULAC cannot depart from its service or civic role, nor can it be a service and political organization at the same time. . . . We cannot reason with opportunists, but we can and we do invite all genuine LULAC [members] to close ranks and continue their service-civic and patriotic pursuits, within the league, in a non-sectarian, non-partisan manner, teaching and defending the democratic principles of INDIVIDUAL political and religious freedom. (Cruz 1969)

The entire notion of increased political activism was shelved that same year at the LULAC national convention. In a resolution filed by Philip Montalvo, the collective membership declared that "the league itself will remain non-political, non-sectarian, and non-partisan" ("Highlights," 1966).

While the attacks on Alfred Hernández were severe, assertions that LULAC should completely refrain from direct political activity would become fewer and farther between. In fact, the older, more conservative members of the league were able to rebuke Hernández but could not garner the necessary votes to have him impeached. Political and demographic shifts changed the character of the group, and by the mid-1960s the Mexican American generation was no longer the driving force in LULAC. Many of the original members had retired from active involvement in politics, and those who remained were beginning to question the need for the group to continue its civil rights activities. Members of the old guard who remained active in LULAC grew disenchanted with the increasingly liberal tone of their group's policies and rhetoric.

During the late 1950s, LULAC had attracted a new cadre of activists, one generation removed from the reformist atmosphere of

World War II. By the mid-1960s, Alfred Hernández was able to articulate a new ideological strain in the organization, one more in keeping with the increased activism of the times. Indeed, he framed the problem clearly when he asked:

> What does it take? What must we do? While I do not condone violence, it may be that we too should resort to marches, sit-ins, and demonstrations. . . . Our government officials are hiding behind the pretext that appointments cannot be had because they cannot find qualified persons of Mexican American extraction to fill positions on the policy making level. . . . *We do have qualified people, but we are being denied our fair share in government, employment, housing, and education.* (A. J. Hernández 1966)

As an organization, LULAC stood at a developmental crossroads. It could cease to exist altogether, find a way to coax increased activism out of its membership through its existing set of purposive appeals, or, as our economic model of organizational development would predict, readjust the reward structure so that LULAC could survive. The tenor of the times pressured the group to adopt a new set of ideological guidelines and assume a more aggressive stand, but the weight of twenty years of activism was taking its toll. The organization had established an incentive structure based on the principles of equal opportunity. In the end, the group did not change the fundamentals of its decades-old constitution or aims and purposes. It would have been difficult to inspire LULAC's political veterans to adopt a new set of purposive incentives. As a result, Chicano activists throughout the Southwest would accuse the group of being satisfied with the status quo while LULAC would reiterate its ideology of orderly institutionally prescribed change.

By this time a marked change had occurred. There was no sense of mission, none of the ideological fire that had characterized the LULAC of the 1940s and 1950s. LULAC rhetoric became less strident and communications between the national organization and local councils deteriorated. In 1972, an issue of the group's official magazine was skipped because there were no news articles submitted to the editor ("Message from Dir. Pub.," 1972: 1). Even the yearly LULAC dues were deemed too heavy a burden for some members to bear. In 1967, LULAC's national legal advisor castigated individual councils for not paying their dues to the national office. Many councils attempted to avoid payment of dues through legal technicalities and maneuvering, even though the national legal advisor noted that the group was still totally dependent on the payment of dues for its operation (Armendáriz 1967). The problem had begun three years earlier when several councils initiated a protest against what they believed to be overly high dues sought by the national office. In 1964 when LULAC dues were increased from $6.00 to $9.00 a year, the national office received a stream of protest. The alleged lack of benefits derived for this modest demand was enough to spark harsh criticism from some members. One spokesman for the backlash charged that since the new dues schedule had been in effect, "the standards of service expected from the National office have not improved to any degree. The question is asked: 'What are we getting for our additional money?'" ("Illinois Criticizes National Office," 1964: 3).

The conflict over dues reflected an unwillingness of the general membership to increase the obligations of LULAC membership and an increasing focus on solidary benefits derived from the organization. This growing sentiment was criticized by the group's leadership in the *LULAC News*. The national president was forced to defend the move and noted that the organization's dues were increased in order to further its political and social goals. His displeasure over the protest came in the form of a sharp rebuke. He noted that the increase "caused a near secession from the union in some states by the same delegates who whooped it up in Disneyland when they should have been attending the business meetings" ("The Presidency," 1964: 2).

Behind the rhetoric and conflict was a political organization in decline. Once a major political force in the Mexican American culture, LULAC could no longer inspire its members to invest their time and energy in the organization, much less create a cohesive political strategy. The mid to late 1960s marked the period in which more signs of decline would appear and the group's leadership would openly discuss the organization's inertia and plot strategies for its revival. But there were marked changes in the character of LULAC as solidary rewards began to play a larger and more important part of the group's incentive structure. Local councils sponsored more dances and banquets, and the national convention became less and less of a forum from which to articulate a political platform and more of an opportunity for the members to enjoy a vacation (Fraga 1980: 50). Critiques of this trend on the part of the leadership circle abounded. Paul Garza, Jr. (president, 1970–71) noted that LULAC was more concerned with its internal affairs than those of the larger community (P. Garza 1964: 7). Others urged the group to shake its image of being the Mexican American Rotary Club and reassert its role as the leader of the civil rights movement for Mexican Americans (A. J. Hernández 1967: 10). Pete V. Villa (national president, 1971–72) argued that LULAC in the early 1970s had become a social rather than an issue-based organization and called upon all LULAC members "to reevaluate ourselves and our endeavors" (Villa 1971). He would later note that LULAC had indeed become the Mexican American Rotary Club. Even the election of top officials in the organization hinged upon personal appeal and friendship networks rather than political or even "civic" issues. He recalled that the debates surrounding his election as national president in 1971 revolved around such matters as the lack of LULAC pins or the publication of *LULAC News*. If LULAC were to address public policy matters it would be at the initiative of the leadership. As Mr. Villa later recalled, his campaign platform for the LULAC presidency centered on internal LULAC issues. In his words, "I got into outside issues after I was elected" (Villa 1986).

The Shift to Government Grants

A major hypothesis in the incentive theory literature states that an organization can mobilize its members on the basis of expressive and purposive interests in its early stage. However, in the long run, a less demanding set of obligations must be devised. One major failure of LULAC from this perspective was that it never offered material incentives to its membership. In order to compensate for the lack of material rewards, it lessened the demands on those members who remained by increasing its dependence on outside support. The political climate of the 1960s and the availability of federal monies for social programs provided the organization with a unique opportunity to become involved in several government programs. While the organization appeared to be much more involved in political activity than ever, much of the increased activism was fueled by an active leadership cadre and an influx of outside monies. Government funding would mask an evolving exchange relationship between the leadership and followers which centered upon providing a number of social activities in exchange for a decreasing amount of issue participation (typically fund raising and ceremonial activities) (Walker 1983).

LULAC did change, but it did so by renegotiating the exchange relationship so that LULAC membership demanded less of an individual's time and effort. The leadership assumed a dominant role in directing the goals and activities of the group, and social activities became a bigger part of LULAC life. As far as the level of membership activity was concerned, the status quo triumphed. The organization would have continued in a state of decline were it not for the explosion of government-sponsored social service programs that became available during the mid-1960s. It would be the Chicano movement's antiestablishment thrust that made groups like LULAC more acceptable to ruling circles than brown power advocates. Mario García (1989: 111) notes that middle-class activists, whose goals were steeped in integration and pluralism, reaped political benefits during the 1960s and 1970s as the establishment sought out less threatening leaders from the Mexican American community. LULAC was ideal in this sense. It was one of the few Mexican American organizations with a national network, a respectable membership (largely middle class), and a tradition of political moderation. It was also one of the few Hispanic groups with a leadership sophisticated enough to deal with public money application procedures (Fraga 1980: 47).

A new group of individuals who would spearhead LULAC's entry into federally sponsored social service programs assumed leadership positions. Individuals like William Bonilla, Roberto Ornelas, Hector Godínez, and Pete Villa began to figure prominently in LULAC activities. The leadership core would invoke the LULAC name to secure funding for a variety of LULAC social service programs in the areas of employment, housing, legal aid, and education. It would be the availability of money for social programs in the late 1960s that would save LULAC from extinction. The leadership core used the LULAC name and reputation to secure millions of dollars in private and government grants. The practical result for LULAC would be a new lease on life. Not only could the group become involved in a variety of activities that would benefit Mexican Americans, it could do so without increasing the burdens on the general membership. The stage was set for the development of a leadership or staff organization.

The first major step in this direction was initiated by George Roybal and Roberto Ornelas, two LULAC members employed by the federal government. Early in 1964, both men sought to create a LULAC-sponsored employment program in which the league would serve as a clearinghouse through which employers involved with government contracts could seek out skilled Hispanic workers and contractors. With the authorization of LULAC's national board of directors, LULAC established employment banks in Houston, Corpus Christi, and Beaumont, Texas. Each was designed to work with the U.S. Navy's Equal Employment Office (Ornelas 1986; Clark 1965: 4). The league's employment banks met with such success that LULAC, along with the GI Forum, sought funding for a five-state research and demonstration project. In early 1966, the Office of Equal Opportunity and the Department of Labor awarded the two organizations $360,000 to establish Project SER (Service, Employment, and Retention). The money would be used to pay for a staff and create a regional office in Albuquerque, New Mexico (Ornelas 1986; Clark 1965: 17).

Soon other projects funded by the federal government or other outside agencies bore the LULAC name. In 1962, the group sponsored its first two government-funded housing projects, Park South Village in San Antonio and Villa Del Norte in El Paso, Texas (Valdez 1969). This two hundred–apartment complex would be the first of several housing projects built in LULAC's flurry of activity in the mid to late 1960s. Another would be built in San Antonio in 1972. Other projects included three in Corpus Christi, one in 1968 and two others in 1971. One other would be built in Kingsville, Texas, in 1972. From 1964 to 1973, LULAC had sponsored six housing projects worth over $17,992,000 (P. Garza 1973).

In 1968 attorney Pete Tijerina, LULAC Texas state civil rights chairman, along with other LULAC leaders, traveled to New York to meet with Ford Foundation officials to discuss the formation of a Mexican American legal defense fund (Oliveira 1978: 9–10). That year a $2.2 million start-up grant from the Ford Foundation established the Mexican American Legal Defense and Educational Fund (MALDEF), a legal aid society. MALDEF's programs and litigation on behalf of Mexican Americans have since been funded by the Ford Foundation and grants from the federal government (O'Connor and Epstein 1984). The fourth area of activity that LULAC engaged in during the early 1970s was education. Although education has always been a prime focus of the organization, government aid in the 1970s allowed LULAC to greatly expand the scope of its activities. In 1973, LULAC received money from the Office of Economic Opportunity to establish LULAC National Education Service Center, Inc. (LNESC). The program was developed to help disadvantaged students receive counseling and technical assistance for enrolling in postsecondary educational institutions. By 1977, the LNESC was funded by the Department of Education with a budget of $1.3 million and operated twelve field centers in communities throughout the United States (Fraga 1980: 47–48).

As our model of organizational development would predict, the pace of the leadership's activity continued to accelerate in the early 1970s. LULAC officials became increasingly involved in government programs, and the LULAC name would be associated with dozens of community programs throughout the Southwest. Encouraged by their successes in these areas, the leadership core attempted an ill-advised membership expansion. This new initiative began in 1973, when Joseph Benetes was elected LULAC national president. His agenda included the increased participation of the organization in government programs, and he urged all local councils to approach all levels of government as well as private corporations for grant monies. His platform emphasized a return to the political activism that characterized the group in the 1950s (Benetes 1974: 9). During his tenure, he attempted to "modernize" the league by establishing a full-time staff and computerizing its operations. The hallmark of his administration was an attempt to make personal contact with all LULAC chapters to "create a truly national organization" and to call upon all members to become actively involved in all LULAC activities. Under his direction, LULAC underwent its first major effort to expand its membership, significantly increase its cash flow, and increase the level of participation among its members (Fraga 1980: 78).

Benetes and his advisors believed that there was still a market within the organization and in the community for the reformism that the group had been advocating for forty-four years. He gambled on this assumption and began borrowing money in order to hire employees for the national office, rent office equipment, and publish a professionally edited *LULAC News*. "Now we believe it makes good sense to undergo a face lifting. If we continue to look poor we're going to think poor and we're long past the time for that kind of attitude" (J. García 1973). His primary goal in this regard was to attract new members and reactivate those already on the membership rolls. However, it is significant that Joe Benetes felt there was a need for a full-time paid staff to coordinate and publicize the efforts of the league. In a way it was a recognition of the constraints that LULAC faced after forty-five years of existence. When asked to comment on the viability of the group functioning with volunteers he argued the obvious: "Volunteers don't have the time or the money to do the same job as a professional staff" ("Just Who," 1973: 5).

The most important point to note about the Benetes revitalization plan was that it repeated the same political ideology and set of values that had failed to nourish the group for years, that of integration and equal opportunity. Indeed, he made a weak case for the existence of prejudice and discrimination or even basic differences between Hispanics and Anglo Americans. For a man who wished to inspire people to enlist in a cause, it was curious to hear him paint a picture of society that emphasized the social and economic similarities between the races. Noting that the two groups were close in their thinking on most issues, he observed that "if I'm living in the same neighborhood as someone else and driving a car that is as nice as his, if our kids go to the same school and our wives shop at the same store, do you really think that we're [Anglos and Mexican Americans] going to be too far apart in our thinking?" ("Just Who," 1973). These were weak purposive incentives, hardly enough to inspire a crusading spirit. Indeed, why join LULAC at all if Mexican Americans now have "their own country clubs, banks, restaurants, night clubs, corporations, law offices, medical centers and serve on civic and charitable boards and enjoy responsible positions in large Anglo-dominated corporations" ("A History of LULAC," 1974: 9)?

In the end nothing came of his effort to attract new membership, and the increase in income they would bring with them did not materialize. These developments assumed a greater significance in light of the delicate relationship between LULAC leaders and the general membership that had developed over the years. Benetes envisioned an increase in funds through increased participation in governmental programs and through increased membership dues. In the end, Benetes' efforts came to naught; neither increased government grants nor membership dues materialized. Office machinery had been purchased, offices rented, and employees hired, but without a new inflow of cash, the organization was dragged into debt for over $200,000. He was subsequently indicted by the LULAC Supreme Council for mismanagement of funds and impeached by the general organization.

Benetes' bold experiment resulted in disaster. The rapid expansion of activities that LULAC experienced from the mid-1960s to the early 1970s came to a sudden halt, and the group was left in disarray. The series of loans and debts incurred by Joseph Benetes were a result of his poor judgment, but they also belied the assertedly good state of the organization. As the group sought to bolster its image before private and government funding agencies, it began to claim an active membership of over 100,000. In reality LULAC in the 1970s was a small group. One portion of the debt was settled out of court for $10,000 in 1975, but the league did not have enough money to pay even that small sum. Subsequently, LULAC was taken back to court and forced to pay the full amount of the original debt (Peña 1986). Because creditors doubted that the organization would assume responsibility for the Benetes debts, the Internal Revenue Service had placed a lien on the homes and properties of several LULAC national leaders. The LULAC expansion program came to a sudden halt, and for the next six years LULAC would be preoccupied with making payments on the $200,000 debt. LULAC came as close as it ever had to declaring bankruptcy and disbanding. As one former national president put it, "We had to regroup."

The Increase in Corporate Support

One result of the debt crisis was to further the process of bureaucratization as well as increase LULAC's dependence on outside sources of income. This time the options for the organization were clear. Either membership dues and income from fund-raising activities would have to increase (representing an increase in demands on the membership) or outside sources of money would have to be found. Many in the organization suggested that LULAC declare bankruptcy and be done with it. The leadership core resisted the temptation and fought for the group's continuity. The group's leaders embarked upon an emergency campaign to raise money from the private and public sectors. As their national president expressed it, "I went around begging for money" (M. González 1986).

Ironically, it would be one of Joseph Benetes' innovations that would serve as a vehicle through which LULAC would attempt to solve its financial problems. During his short tenure as president, he had worked to establish a foundation through which the organization could solicit monies from corporations, and on July 2, 1974, LULAC was granted tax-exempt status for the purpose of corporate contributions (LULAC Foundation, 1978). It seemed like the ideal solution. The creation of the LULAC Foundation could not only tap a new source of income, it could also expand its activities in a way that did not increase material demands on the rank-and-file membership.

The leadership placed their hopes in the new entity, and three years after the creation of the foundation, LULAC used it to aggressively seek corporate support. The establishment of a continuous outreach for corporate support started in 1977 when the Adolph Coors Foundation gave the LULAC Foundation $50,000 to establish an operational office in Denver, Colorado. Shortly thereafter, the LULAC Foundation began to experience some modest successes. The number of corporations that were contributing to the LULAC Foundation increased from five in 1977 to twenty-one in 1979; nineteen were added in the first half of 1980. Still, the foundation's achievements were modest. From 1976 to 1980, the LULAC Foundation funneled over $67,000 directly to the LULAC National Office and an additional $63,000 into various LULAC projects and activities (LULAC Foundation 1980).

The LULAC Foundation seemed to provide an ideal vehicle through which the organization's elite could increase their activities in a relatively painless manner. But its real significance lay in its functional relationship to LULAC itself. Because of legal restrictions placed upon charitable trusts, the LULAC Foundation required a separate bureaucracy, one that would not be under the direct control of the national one. Nevertheless, it would be run by the LULAC elite, those seeking to save the parent organization from financial ruin. The LULAC Foundation's board of directors consisted of the current LULAC national president and others selected from a list of past national presidents (LULAC Foundation n.d.).

The LULAC Foundation was a creation of the LULAC leadership core, and it very quickly assumed the character and operational mode of its parent organization. It was an independent organization, divorced from the direct control of the general membership and consumed by a constant struggle to survive. In 1977, the $12,000 donated by the foundation to various LULAC projects (both national and local) only represented 13 percent of the $94,000 it received in total corporate contributions. The irony of the LULAC Foundation's first year of operation was that it, too, found itself in a financial bind. That year the LULAC Foundation ran a deficit of over $15,000 (LULAC Foundation 1977/78). Although by 1982 the LULAC Foundation had shown a small surplus, the organization had received $107,972 in contributions, yet disbursed only $26,134 in total grants (LULAC Foundation 1982a). One auditor's report found the costs of fund raising were inordinately high in relationship to the total income of the foundation and in 1982 did not meet the standards recognized by organizations that monitor philanthropic groups (LULAC Foundation, 1982a).

The disappointment and frustration the leadership core experienced with the LULAC Foundation led to some harsh intraelite squabbling. So much of the corporate contributions were eaten up by administrative costs that activists accused the LULAC Foundation of acting independently of LULAC and refusing to allocate monies to the national organization. At one point in 1982, Tony Bonilla, LULAC national president, called upon the LULAC Foundation to "cease and desist from raising funds in the name of the LULAC . . . until the matter of cost overruns and grant disbursement was discussed" (T. Bonilla 1982b). The director of the LULAC Foundation defended its policies and argued that because the foundation was "a new entity, it had to encounter growing pains. . . . While money has been available [for distribution], there are stringent rules that must satisfy the 501 3c" IRS restrictions (T. Bonilla 1982a).

The conflicts that existed between the LULAC leadership and the LULAC Foundation were symptomatic of the group's organizational structure. The foundation, like the other major areas of activism that the group became involved in, eventually spawned self-perpetuating bureaucracies, each with its own professional staff. One past president charged that LULAC-sponsored programs had become "Frankensteins," totally independent of and unresponsive to the national organization. In 1984, Arnold Torres, LULAC executive director, decried the lack of control that the LULAC national organization had over its three major programs. Of the LNESC, he noted that it "has never established the proper and efficient ties with the National organization" and that "it is not the policy of the LNESC to properly orient its employees or interns to LULAC, its history and activities." Furthermore, the problem with Project SER, the employment program, was the "independent attitude of its Executive Directors [who] never encourage but discourage cooperation with local LULAC councils." Finally, he charged that the LULAC Foundation, has "failed to raise any significant monies from corporations for the National LULAC Office" (Torres 1984).

However much the failure of the LULAC Foundation to raise money for LULAC troubled the leadership, that failure came as a result of policies which took the burden away from a membership organization unwilling or unable to support those social programs. Project SER, one of the major achievements of LULAC during the late 1960s, encountered serious difficulties early on when LULAC tried to run the job placement program with volunteers. The central problems encountered by LULAC Council 60 in Houston were the lack of expertise and available time volunteers could dedicate to the task. Because of its problem with resources, the volunteer-led program coordinated by the GI Forum and LULAC was placing very few people into jobs. In fact, the program was almost terminated by Council 60 because of its discouraging record (Calderón 1974: 25–26).

The problems that stem from using volunteers to run a service agency are no longer a problem for that particular program. SER Jobs for Progress has been operated on funds provided by the federal government since 1966. By 1985, SER had established a network made up of ninety-six programs located across the United States. Each affiliate had its own paid staff and, in larger cities, satellite offices (*SER Network Directory* 1985). SER also held its own annual convention, conducted its own corporate fund-raising drives, and, in 1981, constructed its own national headquarters in Dallas, Texas (*SER Annual Report* 1982). Although SER is run by a LULAC and

GI Forum board of directors, for all practical purposes it has long ceased to depend on LULAC for organizational direction and financial support.

The only LULAC organization which still was subject to a degree of control by LULAC leaders and the general membership was the LNESC. In 1983, $238,678 was raised by local councils for the LNESC scholarship fund. In all, fifty-nine local councils in forty-nine cities and seventeen states participated in fund-raising activities (LULAC Board of Directors 1983). Corporate support almost doubled the amount contributed by the LULAC general membership. A total of fifty corporations pledged $546,207, and almost $1 million in federal funds were allocated to the LNESC for operating expenses in 1983. In total, government grants constituted over 64 percent of the total revenue for the LNESC (LNESC 1983). While the local LULAC councils themselves may have raised a substantial sum of money, their overall contribution to the program was small and even this program had drifted away from LULAC control and influence. With its outside sources of money and semiautonomous bureaucratic structure, there was little reason for the LNESC to be held accountable to LULAC itself. This attitude is reflected in the LNESC staff. One local director of an LNESC branch office recalled that when he started his job he wondered when he would be asked to join LULAC. When the matter was raised with his supervisor, he was told that "it was not necessary."

Exchange and Equilibrium

Exchange theory predicts that member participation in an organization will decline and it becomes the job of the leadership to redefine the exchange relationship within the group to maintain a minimal level of participation. The pattern of decreased membership, less direct membership participation in organization activities, and an increasingly important role taken by the leadership elite became evident from the early to the late 1960s. In 1951, LULAC had a membership of 2,500, which grew to 3,300 in 1952. But in 1964, when the organization began its program of expanded activism, LULAC reported the number had dropped to under 2,000; in 1968 at the peak of LULAC's involvement in government-sponsored programs, membership remained at just under 2,000.[1] Although the LULAC leadership core was involved in several multimillion-dollar service programs and its reputation had been enhanced, membership was actually dwindling. There were few jobs to be obtained through LULAC membership, and throughout LULAC's activist period, the organization failed to develop other material incentives for members. Most LULAC work was still strictly voluntary. Actual income generated from within the group (dues, fees, fund raising, etc.) was less than $17,000 in the period from 1965 to 1969 (Vásquez 1968). These dismal figures prompted the group's business manager to note that at best, membership was holding steady, but compared to the group's involvement in government sponsored programs, LULAC itself was a "horse and buggy organization" (Vásquez 1968).

Interestingly, membership did eventually grow after the Benetes debacle. Succeeding LULAC national presidents made an effort to increase membership and create new councils throughout the Southwest and the nation. Their efforts were largely successful and by 1982 there were just under 5,000 dues-paying members in the organization. However, this increase in membership reflected the energy with which the leadership promoted the development of new councils to help pay the Benetes-incurred debt and the social benefits to be derived from membership rather than a sense of dedication to collective goals. By the 1980s LULAC was larger than ever before, but the national organization was resting on a fragile and unreliable membership base. Although local councils have traditionally exercised a great degree of autonomy, the relationship between the national headquarters and LULAC councils across the Southwest was tenuous indeed. In 1982, the national office reported that membership accounting procedures and communication between the national office and local councils were "in a state of stagnation and chaos" (Altman 1982).

While the organization had more members than at any other point in its history, their ties to LULAC were weak. In March 1985, the LULAC membership coordinator lamented the fact that of 335 LULAC councils on their books, only 20 had paid their dues for that year and a total of 134 councils had not paid their dues for the past five years (D. Hernández 1985b). Even the minimum amount of communication between the local and the national offices was lacking. In an appeal to LULAC state and district directors, the national membership coordinator pleaded for the most basic data on local membership. Few responded to this query, which resulted in the national office not knowing whether its mailing lists were incorrect, if local leaders were still in office, or whether local councils had disbanded (D. Hernández 1985a).

Thus, while membership grew, the group did not exercise a strong grip on their loyalties. Many individuals would be enticed to join and pay their dues and initiation fees only to leave the group a short time later. This process pointed to a breakdown in the traditional structure of rewards in the organization. The "chaos" in accounting procedures and communications networks reported by the LULAC national membership coordinator indicated that many councils were not viable and their members did not care to pay their dues or invest enough time to maintain a minimum of contact with the national organization. In some areas of the Southwest, councils were disbanding as quickly as new ones could be formed.

Such problems would cripple the efforts of any organizational network to act in a concerted fashion. Nevertheless, there is evidence of widespread satisfaction on the part of the general membership with LULAC's existing system of demands and rewards. In a survey of the membership commissioned by LULAC, the most important problems facing the organization were cited as (in order of importance) communication between the national office and local councils, issues clarification, funding, lack of unity, and a diminishing membership (Boone 1983: 3). The major complaint members had with the organization did not center on policy concerns but on a lack of information concerning the group's functioning or the actions of their leadership (Boone 1983: 13). At the same time, the membership was generally satisfied with the status quo. A full 66 percent expressed satisfaction with the overall performance of LULAC and only 18 percent expressed dissatisfaction. Similar percentages were also registered when the rank and file evaluated the national leadership and its ability to fulfill LULAC goals (Boone 1983: 2).

Through the 1970s and 1980s the national leadership criticized all four LULAC-initiated entities for their independence and lack of responsiveness to the central office. LULAC members generally expressed a great deal of support for two quasi-LULAC entities, the LNESC and Project SER. Fifty-nine percent of all LULAC members polled approved of the LNESC's performance, and 60 percent approved of Project SER. It should be reiterated that these were projects that required little or no input or sacrifice from the individuals who overwhelmingly approved of their performance. Only the LULAC Foundation, which had thus far failed to secure significant amounts of monies for LULAC, received a low 32 percent approval rating (32 percent expressed disapproval, with the others offering no opinion or a neutral evaluation) (Boone 1983: 5–6).

LULAC members generally expressed more satisfaction with the overall operation of their local councils than with the national office, even though there was a great degree of ambivalence toward both. Substantial numbers of the membership expressed neither wholly negative nor positive attitudes toward the national organization, and members were also divided in their assessment of the local council's role in the community or its effectiveness in helping the Hispanic community (Boone 1983: 2). Not surprisingly, many members expressed concern that their organization had no clear-cut goals or objectives; many felt that even the local leadership was not responsive to membership demands. However, only a small minority ever expressed great dissatisfaction with the organization or its independent agencies.

These doubts and contradictory opinions concerning the organization did not indicate great unrest within the group. There was every indication that members were generally satisfied with the organizational status quo and were strongly opposed to increasing the costs of participation. When asked where LULAC should focus its fund-raising efforts, the membership were almost unanimous in voicing an opposition to increasing their own costs of participation. A full 58 percent suggested that the organization seek monies from the private sector, 10 percent suggested the federal government, and 20 percent suggested special fund-raising events (dances, festivals, etc.). Only 6 percent of the members surveyed suggested that LULAC raise additional funds through increased dues. This was true even though 21 percent of all LULAC members had completed graduate school and 56 percent made $20,000 a year or more in 1983, while LULAC membership dues were only $12 a year (Boone 1983: 10).

Over time the exchange relationship within LULAC has centered on fraternal activity and cultural expression. Virtually all LULAC members support this aspect of its activities. As one past president stated, LULAC is a "benevolent association that allows you to retain ties to your culture, history, and ethnic origins." However, the political role that LULAC should be playing was never clearly defined. LULAC's aims and purposes restrict the organization's scope of activities to those civic in nature or what might be called "community service to your fellow Hispanics." During the 1950s, this statement was generally understood to mean that LULAC was committed to the achievement of formal equality for Mexican Americans. As the organization aged and the barriers to formal equality were done away with, the consensus that united the group broke down. With the passing away of the most blatant forms of discrimination against Mexican Americans, the more tenacious problems of poverty and powerlessness called for solutions that went beyond LULAC's traditional commitment to equal opportunity. Thus, the vague formula that committed the LULAC membership to serving the Hispanic community no longer generated a consensus over goals or tactics.

Since the early 1960s, LULAC had been plagued by confusion over the organization's purpose and policies, and the members themselves were divided over the purpose the organization should serve. The great majority of the membership are comfortable with a broad mandate for the organization. When queried, 61 percent believe that LULAC should be a "civic," nonpolitical organization. Those that believe the group should become politically active constitute a small minority. Only 6 percent believed that LULAC is a political organization or should become involved in politics. On the other hand, a full 24 percent believed the group is a social organization (Boone 1983: 2). The problem was aptly summarized by one past president: "LULAC has to be everything. We provide fraternity. It is also a patriotic organization, its preamble and motto are built on [developing] A-1 citizens. Finally it is issue oriented" (P. Garza 1986).

Conclusion

This chapter has argued that LULAC faced the problem of maintaining membership support after the initial wave of activism of the 1950s had subsided. LULAC evolved from an activist organization into one that was largely detached from its members and dependent on outside sources to fund its activities. Shortly after World War II, all the time devoted to LULAC fund drives, litigation, and pressure tactics was initiated by volunteers. The league did not pay its officers, lawyers, or any other individual acting in the name of the group. However, ethnic or minority organizations are not immune from the problems of declining membership interest, the establishment of a leadership core, and the accompanying dependence upon outside sources of funding. An organization as old and well-established in Mexican American politics as LULAC was still faced with the necessity of formulating a set of tangible rewards that would satisfy its existing membership base as well as attract others to the fold. LULAC's solution was to lessen the material costs on its members by reaching out to the federal government and the private sector for financial support as well as to increase the amount of solidary and expressive (symbolic) benefits to its members.

LULAC's ideology and expressive incentives lost much of their power in the late 1950s. The conservative ideology of the group prompted many of its members to restrict the number of hours they were willing to contribute after many of the goals they had set for themselves seemed to have been achieved. For the LULAC old guard, the political element in the original exchange relationship had been negotiated and achieved. Indeed, for many of the World

War II generation of LULAC members, the necessity for LULAC as a political organization was rapidly diminishing. Nonetheless, the passage of time and the evolution of the leadership cadre were not the sole factors involved in the bureaucratization of this civil rights organization.

The influx of some politically oriented activists in the late 1950s and early 1960s dramatized the group's problems as they attempted to steer LULAC in a more political direction. The new activists failed to rekindle the activist fervor of LULAC's earlier period and were forced to expand LULAC's activities themselves while reducing an already light burden of participation on the membership. Thus, while the league's public profile grew in the mid-1960s and the group was involved in a wide range of political activities, these events occurred with little mass participation and with a heavy dose of outside financial support. These monies came primarily from the federal government and later from corporations such as Coors Brewing Company and Sears Roebuck. One unforeseen result of this increased dependence on outside funding was the creation of independent agencies with a tenuous or nonexistent relationship to LULAC. LULAC leaders set general policy guidelines for Project SER, the LNESC, and the LULAC Foundation, but these entities had their own bureaucratic structure and professional staff who, on a day-to-day basis, operated independently from the league. The LULAC Foundation, designed to secure monies for the organization's own activities, enjoyed modest success at best. It had to secure enough monies for its own bureaucracy before passing on any funds to its parent organization.

Contemporary membership attitudes suggest that an equilibrium has been reached in demands and expectations in LULAC participation. As shall be demonstrated in the next chapter, not only do LULAC members refuse to increase the demands placed upon themselves, they express a satisfaction with the functioning of the organization and its independent entities. They do not wish to see dues raised to fund group functions and feel satisfied with the group's performance, even though there is no general agreement on its purpose or political role. Indeed, these attitudes, combined with the fact that a full one-fourth of the membership believe that the group is a social group and another 61 percent believe that it is a vaguely defined "civic" organization, suggest that an equilibrium between demands and expectations has been reached among the general membership, and most of the group's struggles involve day-to-day survival.

5. The Politics of Survival

The 1980s would find LULAC's leaders trading on its history and image in the Mexican American community. In addition to applying for gifts and grants from the federal government, the group began seeking pacts and accords with American corporations to increase investment and hiring in the Mexican American community similar to those worked out by the National Association for the Advancement of Colored People (NAACP) and other black organizations. In July 1983, LULAC national president Tony Bonilla in conjunction with other Hispanic and black organizations signed an accord with the Southland Corporation, owners of the 7-Eleven chain of convenience stores and Chief Auto Parts stores. The next year another was signed with the Miller Brewing Company. The open-ended pacts stipulate that these corporations will strive to increase the numbers of minorities hired in their stores, purchase goods and services from minority firms, create special funds for use in joint ventures with prospective minority distributors, and ensure that a fixed percentage of their philanthropic gifts will be contributed to minority organizations (Ortiz 1987: 8–9).

Even though LULAC spent much of its time accommodating itself to the wishes of the private sector, the monies it was able to secure from it were minuscule. In an age of multimillion-dollar PAC contributions and high-cost media campaigns, LULAC is a small, elite group. The small number of members and the tiny budget belie the image of a national Hispanic organization with a sixty-year history. In those sixty years, LULAC traveled a long way down the path of dependence, and the LULAC leadership in the 1980s would be absorbed in a constant search for outside monies. By the time the group entered the 1980s, its dependence on corporate grants was marked, and the amount of corporate monies coming into the LULAC national organization was more than double what it received from dues, initiation fees, and charter fees. In 1979, a little over $50,000 in dues and fees was collected by the national organization and $107,000 was donated by outside sources ("LULAC Income," 1979; "LULAC Statement," 1979). Housing projects, educational agencies, and job-training programs bearing the LULAC name operate with million-dollar budgets and national staffs while LULAC itself is an impoverished organization, dependent upon an unstable membership base for dues and the goodwill of the private sector.

What hard data exist on LULAC membership since the 1950s indicate that the organization's membership reflected the degree of commitment to its political activism.[1] During the 1950s, when purposive and expressive rewards predominated, LULAC was a relatively small group. The general membership at this time grew and remained fairly stable. A roster of all councils in 1948–49 listed forty-nine councils, all of which were in Texas (LULAC 1948–49; LULAC 1949). But by 1952 the group expanded and there were sixty-one councils in three states (LULAC 1952). There was continued growth during these activist years. Membership rolls show that in 1951–52 there were 2,478 paid members in the group, a figure that grew to a post–World War II high of 3,300 in 1952–53. Quite the opposite occurred when the group faced increased difficulty in its desegregation efforts. The white community resisted efforts to implement court-ordered desegregation plans, and LULAC's litigation came to an end in 1957 (San Miguel 1987: 134). The white community's resistance, in conjunction with the growing feeling among LULAC members that racial equality had been achieved, had an adverse impact on the numbers of activists the organization could claim. By the late 1950s membership had dropped to 2,800.

The effectiveness of LULAC's purposive and expressive benefits was further eroded in the decade that followed. As disagreement over the group's purpose became manifest, membership began to drop during the mid-1960s. In 1964–65, the group's total membership had dropped to 1,334, less than half of what it was under the administration of Felix Tijerina (1956–1960). From 1965 to 1969 membership never went above 1,550. By 1972, LULAC could claim only 1,000 members.

The LULAC that emerged in the 1970s was a changed organization. The leadership core had made it easier to become a member of LULAC by lessening the activist demands on its members and by bolstering the group's finances through government grants and private sector gifts. This produced rewards, and in a few short years the LULAC appeal brought in a new set of individuals. By 1977 LULAC membership figures were once again on the upswing. That year

4,167 individuals paid their LULAC dues. This figure remained steady throughout the decade, with a small drop in 1980. However, by the second term of Ruben Bonilla (1981), LULAC membership had reached an all-time high. At that point, LULAC recorded a membership of over 6,300. There was a drop-off after Mr. Bonilla's term, but throughout the 1980s, membership remained steady at about 4,500 (see the chart in the appendix).

LULAC and the Increased Role of Leadership

Over time, LULAC survived because of its ability to lower participation costs and increase solidary rewards. In the process it lost its activist base while succeeding as a bureaucratic, elite-directed group. Today a small group of leaders dominates the national structure while local councils are free to define their own agenda. If they choose to participate in the political process or operate as a social club, they are free to do so. What remains at the national level is a leadership group which sets the "direction" LULAC is to take from year to year and acts as the central organizing committee for dues collection and fund raising.

Although LULAC has become a loose confederation of local councils, it is not without its rewards for the central leadership. When individuals assume leadership roles at the national level in LULAC, they are placed in a position of high visibility and potential influence. No other national, membership-based Mexican American organization can rival LULAC's high profile or claim to speak on behalf of the entire Hispanic community. Given LULAC's history and name recognition in the political community, the actions and utterances of its leadership carry great symbolic weight. If the national president calls a press conference, marches on a picket line, or engages in any other high-profile activity, LULAC is in the news, and the image of a vital and muscular organization is projected by the national media. As one national president remarked, "The media and people in this country look at LULAC as being the spokesperson for Hispanics in the United States. They look at us as being the mouthpiece for Hispanics" (de Lara 1988). Although there are many elected Latino public and organizational leaders with more actual power than a LULAC national president, their constituency is limited or regional in scope. Few other Mexican American leaders can generate a national presence or claim to speak on behalf of all Latinos.

Because of its long history and record of activism in the area of civil rights, LULAC commands a strong symbolic position not only in the Mexican American political community but in the political system as a whole. Since opening an office in Washington, D.C., in 1979, the group has been in a position to issue press releases and communicate with the media. The group has been able to bank on its past in order to speak on any issue affecting Mexican Americans. Nevertheless, the political clout associated with LULAC officialdom does not go farther than the image it is able to project. The organization's councils are independent entities with varying focuses and interests. It is doubtful that the organization could back up its claims and threats with anything resembling mass mobilization on the part of its local councils.

Years of bureaucratization and the general lack of unified action on the part of its members have made what remains of LULAC an organization fueled by the energy and determination of its leadership. Because the membership have little influence over the operation of the national organization, individual national presidents define the goals and ideological direction the group will take. Individuals who are elected to the office of national president find themselves in charge of a malleable organization and can reshape the group's image and policies. The best examples of the leadership defining the group and its position on issues affecting Latinos in the United States came in the late 1970s and 1980s. The election of three outspoken individuals to the LULAC presidency between 1979 and 1985 marked what could be termed the liberal era of LULAC. Ruben Bonilla (1979–1981), Tony Bonilla (1981–1983), and Mario Obledo (1983–1985) were outspoken critics of government policy and sought to bring LULAC back into the forefront of the struggle for social and economic equality for Mexican Americans. During this time, the group's name was often mentioned in the press as its leaders articulated positions on issues from bilingual education to Central America.

After a decade of low-key leadership, it suddenly appeared as if LULAC were blossoming into a new era of aggressive political action. But the appearance of a renewed assertiveness was generated entirely by the activism and personal style of the individuals involved. Ruben Bonilla was tireless in his efforts to advance a progressive agenda for Mexican Americans. In the month he was elected as LULAC national president, he issued a scathing attack on the Carter administration and its neglect of the Mexican American population and its problems. He characterized the alleged neglect as a "slap in the face" which would be remembered at the polls the following year (Noticias 1979). His staff at the LULAC national office compiled a list of areas in which the Carter administration had failed to address the social and economic problems of the Mexican American for circulation to the press and LULAC membership (R. Bonilla ca. 1979). Despite these attacks, though, Bonilla later made the national news by endorsing the president for re-election ("Press Release," 1980). One scholar noted that during Bonilla's tenure as LULAC national president

> he attended more national and international conferences than any other past national president and met with U.S. President Jimmy Carter and Mexican President José López Portillo. He was quick to publicly criticize government policies in the areas of immigration, police community relations, and a number of other issues. His opinion on major issues was publicized in magazines such as the *Texas Monthly, U.S. News and World Report, Politics Today, The Texas Observer, Newsweek*, and *Texas Business*. (Fraga 1980: 82–83)

While Ruben Bonilla had been Texas LULAC state director, he had established Hispanics Organized for Political Education (HOPE), which was supposed to be the political arm of LULAC. HOPE consisted of a national board of directors appointed by LULAC national officials who would engage in voter registration drives and political campaigns (HOPE 1980). The real significance of HOPE was its publicity-generating capacity for LULAC. During Bonilla's term as Texas state director of LULAC, the organization would issue weekly bulletins or position papers on topics ranging from the energy crisis to employment patterns for Hispanics. Bonilla's skillful use of the mass media put LULAC into the national limelight. He later estimated that for every announcement or press release he issued, the national office would receive twenty-five to thirty telephone calls from other groups or elected officials (R. Bonilla, Jr. 1985).

After serving two terms as national president, Ruben Bonilla was succeeded by his brother Tony Bonilla (1981–1983), another liberal, activist LULAC president. He too was determined to bring the organization into the national political arena. He established links with several black organizations, testified before Congress on various issues, and marched with César Chávez in support of the United Farm Workers Union (T. Bonilla 1982a). He also was a vociferous critic of the Reagan administration. During his tenure as national president, Tony Bonilla published several position papers on the impact of Ronald Reagan's economic policies. In one paper, entitled "Reaganomics: A Threat to Internal Security," Bonilla charged that the Reagan administration's economic program was "disastrous to all except wealthy individuals and major corporations" ("Reaganomics," 1983: 5). He was a critic of Reagan's defense build-up and the growing federal deficit ("LULAC Review," 1981).

Mario Obledo was elected to the national presidency after Tony Bonilla and continued his predecessor's tradition of openly criticizing the government. Perhaps his most controversial action as LULAC national president came in 1984 when he led a delegation of LULAC leaders to Cuba. Seeking to gather information and help establish friendlier ties between Cuba and the United States, Obledo's five-person delegation visited hospitals and schools. It also featured private meetings with top Cuban officials, including a four-hour session with Fidel Castro (del Olmo 1984b). The high-profile meeting with Cuban officials angered the Reagan administration, whose representatives refused to meet with Obledo for a first-hand report from LULAC (Olvera 1984). Obledo would further antagonize the Reagan administration by advocating normalization of U.S.-Cuban relations, including the establishment of normal trade relations with the socialist state ("Lulac Report," 1984). One of his final acts as LULAC president was a three-day visit to Nicaragua, where he declared that the newly formed state had elements of democracy and wanted peace (Obledo 1984: 2).

The terms of Ruben Bonilla, Tony Bonilla, and Mario Obledo marked a time when the organization issued a stream of criticisms of the government through the media. The views of these three individuals would be summarized in a report prepared by Arnold Torres, the national executive director. His document, *Economic Analysis Review 1981–84*, was a searing analysis of the Reagan administration's budgetary policies. To the casual observer, LULAC was a strident watchdog of Hispanic interests, and to anyone who read its position papers, press releases, and other communications, the group was a strongly liberal organization with the political muscle to reward its friends and punish its enemies. But as our theoretical model predicts and subsequent events bear out, the flurry of activity and the high profile of the organization were a function of a small group of individuals and their ability to generate publicity. Ruben Bonilla, the most adept at manipulating the media to LULAC's advantage, once suggested that the energies of LULAC's leadership and the modest amount of monies in LULAC's coffers be saved in lieu of attending the yearly American GI Forum convention. He suggested to Tony Bonilla and Arnold Torres that LULAC may "as well realize that the GI Forum Convention is not going to get us any news coverage and will not enable us to make any strong impact in the California Hispanic Community" (R. Bonilla 1980).

Bonilla was an astute political player, as were others in the inner circle of LULAC's leadership. His warning that an overextension of the leadership's commitments would consume LULAC's energy and limited resources was an admission that LULAC depended upon its national leadership to give the organization visibility. In short, if LULAC were to maintain a national recognition, it would come as a result of elite efforts. As a 1981 internal document revealed,

> Much of the organization's tremendous growth and development in this brief period [1979–1981] has been possible because of the personal commitment, charisma, and financial independence of its Immediate Past National President, Ruben Bonilla. However, LULAC as an organization, is ill-equipped to maintain this aggressive profile. Formalized long range planning is lacking. Dues collection, membership services, and communications are not institutionalized systems. In short, LULAC is largely dependent on the selection of future officers, and their willingness to contribute personal and financial resources of a scale needed to sustain the organization's momentum. (LULAC 1981: 3)

This organizational shortcoming would be highlighted in the mid-1980s as a new national president was elected, one with little of the fire and liberalism of his predecessors. If Ruben Bonilla, Tony Bonilla, and Mario Obledo gave LULAC an image and prominence unjustified by its actual strength, one would expect the group to drop from public view or redefine its image once a different kind of individual was elected to head the organization. This was precisely what happened in 1985. When Oscar Morán was elected national president that year, the impressive amount of media coverage LULAC generated during the early 1980s came to an abrupt halt. Mr. Moran was known for his support of Ronald Reagan and the conservative Texas governor William Clements. The *Wall Street Journal*'s coverage of the 1986 national convention made much of the change of leadership in LULAC. It was asserted that after a single election "the group no longer seems so liberal. LULAC has become conspicuously silent on the kind of social and economic issues that once might have prompted a flurry of news releases and lawsuits. Some Hispanic activists charge, far from being liberal, LULAC has become downright conservative" (Moffett 1986: 52).

The era of high-profile liberalism projected by the Bonilla brothers and Mario Obledo was over, but it was not because the organization had suddenly become conservative. There was no groundswell of opposition or discontent with the leadership of these individuals. Indeed, 50 percent of the LULAC membership was satisfied or very satisfied with the national presidency of the outspoken and liberal

Tony Bonilla. Only 26 percent expressed dissatisfaction with his leadership, yet after Bonilla's last term in office, the organization elected Oscar Morán, an individual whose personal style and philosophy were different from Bonilla's in almost every respect (Boone 1983: 5). At the root of the shift was a lack of issue conflict among the general membership. As was noted earlier, LULAC's national presidents, although themselves motivated by social and political concerns, found that the conflicts surrounding their election to LULAC office were based more on personality and friendship ties than on policy issues. The only reason the election of Oscar Morán generated any controversy was because his challenger was Dr. Anita del Río, only the second woman to run for the LULAC national presidency.

Anita del Río ran her candidacy on a platform of immigration reform, bilingual education, and other standard issues but noted that delegates to LULAC national conventions cast their votes according to personal allegiances formed in the past. "That is why you see no debates over issues. They have made up their mind before the convention" (del Río 1986). In this particular election, gender was the major issue discussed. Women comprise more than 50 percent of LULAC membership but hold fewer than 2 percent of the elected positions. Indeed, in a survey of LULAC members, virtually all female respondents felt that Hispanic males would not support women in leadership positions and that Hispanic culture has a negative influence on the election of women to such posts (Boone 1983: 4). As del Río would later assert, "Texas men are terribly proud." To have a woman in a leadership role "would be humiliating to them" (del Río 1986).

The issue of gender was the underlying cause of the lopsided two-to-one defeat del Río suffered. It appeared to be the only issue that raised significant concern. On all substantive issues there was little difference between the two candidates' platforms. When Oscar Morán ran for the LULAC national presidency he vowed to work on economic development in the community and civil rights and to fight the Simpson-Mazolli immigration reform bill, a platform virtually identical to that of del Río (Quintanilla 1985). But after his election, the new national president followed precedent and began to mold LULAC into an organization following his own political views. National president Morán promised to work for closer ties with the corporate sector, desist from the "confrontational style" of past presidents, and halt LULAC's attacks on President Reagan (Scharrer 1985a). His belief was that this strategy was necessary so as to avoid creating "negative feelings and bad blood"

(Scharrer 1985b). The conservative president refrained from criticizing the Reagan administration and the effect of Reagan's policies on Mexican Americans. These years would be what del Río called a "honeymoon" for the Reagan administration (del Río 1986).

During this time, LULAC was seen by other community activists as remaining silent on important policy questions concerning Mexican Americans (Moffett 1986). But the honeymoon Ronald Reagan received from Morán did not seem to disturb many of the rank-and-file members. This attitude of complacency was indicative of an uninterested general membership, especially since Morán's election represented a marked shift in the leadership's political ideology. The Bonilla years were marked by constant criticism of the government, and Mario Obledo condemned Ronald Reagan's foreign policy in Central America (Moffett 1986). But by the time Oscar Morán was elected national president, LULAC had long since passed its activist stage of development. Despite the fact that Morán represented a reversal of the liberal trend set in the early to mid-1980s, no significant challenge to his policies would be mounted. Furthermore, he would be elected to three consecutive one-year terms with virtually no opposition, more years in office than any other LULAC president since Felix Tijerina (1956–1960).

It is not clear how much this shift away from a strident liberal tone created difficulties for other members of the leadership core. The only individual to openly bridle at the new tone of LULAC politics was Arnold Torres, the outspoken LULAC executive director under Ruben and Tony Bonilla and Mario Obledo. Torres resigned his position in 1984 after the LULAC national board voted to support the nomination of Edwin Meese to the post of U.S. attorney general (Moffett 1986). His frustration with the status of LULAC was evident when he argued that "the Republicans on the board are concerned more with placating the White House than in really advocating for the community. I wanted a program of aggressive advocacy. I wanted a lean, mean fighting machine. Just look at what it's done recently: nothing. The letters to the Hill have not gone out. The lobbying hasn't taken place. The strong advocacy has not been there. That speaks for itself" ("Torres Resigns," 1985: 9).

Among other members of the leadership elite, there was little conflict over the shift in emphasis. Even Ruben Bonilla, the liberal stalwart of the late 1970s, remarked that the country was "going through a period of intense conservatism, and LULAC is not immune [to national shifts]," that the election of a conservative president for LULAC was a step forward, and that Oscar Morán was "the right man in the right place at the right time" (Scharrer 1985b).

The Politics of Economic Dependence

When a group moves beyond the initial stage of mobilization, its elite spends more and more time insuring the group's continued existence; normative and political concerns begin to take a back seat to the fund-raising cycle. One of the most controversial steps LULAC's leaders took in their fund-raising efforts was to accept money from the Adolph Coors Brewing Company. The public association with Coors not only brought them into direct conflict with other Mexican American organizations but pointed to the difficulty that LULAC found itself in. The Adolph Coors Company's union-busting campaigns, discriminatory hiring practices, and support for the Nicaraguan Contras led to a nationwide effort on the part of Mexican American organizations and other liberal groups to boycott the company's products (Acuña 1988: 380). Given the pressures experienced by the organization, LULAC had little choice. While the Coors Brewing Company was linked with antiminority and conservative causes, LULAC had found a patron who was willing to donate money to the insolvent organization.

The relationship LULAC had with Coors and other companies was a relationship born of necessity. Even though LULAC was raising more outside monies than ever and had established ties to a wide range of companies, the organization itself was constantly teetering on the brink of financial disaster. In 1981, six years after Joseph Benetes had driven the organization into disarray, LULAC still owed $160,000 of the original $200,000 debt (LULAC National Office Balance Sheet, December 31, 1981). At the end of the 1982 fiscal year little progress had been made, and the organization owed the Banco Internacional de Tucson $154,000 and American Express $6,000 incurred during the Benetes administration (LULAC 1983).

In spite of a steady infusion of corporate money into its coffers, the national organization was still jumping from one crisis to the next. In 1983 LULAC once again came close to declaring bankruptcy. Through a gross miscalculation of incoming monies, LULAC experienced a severe financial crisis, and the organization was forced to lay off most of its staff in Washington, D.C. National president Tony Bonilla ordered the Washington office to give a leave of absence to all its staff except for the LULAC executive director, one assistant, and a secretary; eliminate all travel; prioritize all debts; and make contact with corporations to seek additional financial support (T. Bonilla 1983). The national LULAC office was operating on a budget of $10,000 per month, and only $50,000 to $60,000 in dues was expected for the entire year (Villarreal 1983). Given this level of dependency, it is doubtful that LULAC could mount much of a campaign against corporations charged with discriminatory hiring practices even if it was so inclined.

Coors may have been an emotionally charged symbol of corporate arrogance among Mexican American political activists, but LULAC made peace with the company early on. On August 29, 1974, LULAC national president Joe Benetes announced that LULAC would end its support of a boycott against the Coors Brewing Company of Golden, Colorado. One of the primary reasons the boycott against Coors products began in 1969 was because of discriminatory hiring practices against Mexican Americans and the company's opposition to a union drive. Nevertheless, Benetes stated that LULAC conducted a complete investigative study of Coors' plant operations and there was no reason to boycott the company's products ("LULAC Ends," 1974). That announcement, which came more than fourteen years before the national boycott of Coors ended, marked the beginning of a close relationship between LULAC and Coors. Beginning with a $50,000 grant in 1977 for the creation of the LULAC Foundation, Coors has funneled thousands of dollars into the LULAC Foundation and the LULAC national office. Over the years, the group deepened its involvement with Coors. In 1984, LULAC was one of six national Latino organizations that signed a five-year agreement with Coors. Under the terms of the agreement, the company agreed to hire more Hispanics and donate a minimum of $2.5 million to Hispanic organizations, provided that sales of its products increased among Hispanics between 1985 and 1990 (Ortiz 1987: 10). While the wisdom of promoting beer consumption among a population plagued by social and economic deprivation is dubious, the lure of corporate monies was overwhelming. When Joseph Benetes announced the termination of the beer boycott in 1974, he also mentioned the possibility of LULAC itself obtaining a Coors distributorship ("LULAC Ends," 1974).

This relationship did not come without its price for the organization. Because of its public support for the company, LULAC came under the most severe criticism it had experienced since the late 1960s (del Olmo 1984a). Not only was LULAC attacked by other Mexican American groups, it received criticism from a wide array of groups opposed to Coors Brewing Company's support for a number of conservative political causes. LULAC national president Tony Bonilla (1981–1983) was well aware of the obligations LULAC incurred when it accepted Coors monies and the awkward position his group was placed in when making its yearly solicitation for funds. In a letter to Joseph Coors he emphasized how much LULAC valued its relationship with the Coors Company, but "because we have received this charity from your company, we have been effectively neutralized and in the process we are looked upon by some sources as 'vendidos' [sell-outs]. Furthermore, we have found it necessary from time to time to defend our position and in the process to defend your organization against attacks made by other groups" (T. Bonilla 1983).

The Adolph Coors Company was very conscious of what it was purchasing with its contributions. Coors kept the LULAC national leaders informed of any attempt by LULAC councils or any other group to back the Coors boycott. They were also informed of specific instances when the direct intervention of the national office was necessary. In 1982, the AFL-CIO was stepping up its campaign against Coors products and was lobbying local LULAC councils in Chicago and California to lend their support to the boycott. Shortly afterward, the national office was informed by a Coors representative that the efforts to recruit local LULAC councils to help with the boycott was having a detrimental effect on the company. Coors representatives noted that "the unions are suggesting that LULAC still regards Coors to be anti-minority among other things." Coors wanted something done about it, and the national president of LULAC was asked to try to devise "a possible solution" (S. Martínez 1982).

The ties were drawn even closer in 1984 when LULAC, along with the American GI Forum, the Cuban National Planning Council, the National Council of La Raza, National Image, Inc., and the U.S. Hispanic Chamber of Commerce, signed an economic development agreement with Coors. In exchange for promoting Coors products among Latinos, Coors would reinvest a portion of its profits in the community. However, in this case, LULAC council 2858 in Garden Grove, California, broke away from the national directive and urged a continued boycott of Coors products. They charged that Coors engaged in a number of anti-Latino activities such as discriminatory hiring practices; the "collaboration with police brutality" in Denver; union busting; support for the conservative think tank, the Heritage Foundation; and contributions to groups such as the Moral Majority and the John Birch Society. They characterized the national organization's acceptance of money from Coors as "tantamount to receiving money from Safeway or Lucky's during the prolonged UFW [grape] boycotts" (Camacho and López 1984). The California LULAC district 1 quickly issued a press release as soon as the conflict became public, reaffirming the national organization's support of the Coors Brewing Company. A directive to the errant council was issued, ordering the Garden Grove council and all LULAC members to "cease and desist in voicing statements contrary to LULAC National, State and District Policies" ("LULAC District," 1984). That year, the Adolph Coors Company would award a $2,000 grant to the California LULAC district for the league scholarship program during the second annual state ball ("60th Attend," 1984: 15).

The uncomfortable relationship LULAC has with Coors is a manifestation of its dependence on outside monies for its day-to-day operations. But over the years, corporate America has been injecting a steady stream of outside funds into LULAC's social events as well. Not only have corporate monies made the day-to-day operation of the organization possible while limiting the need for the rank and file to contribute to the national treasury, they have found their way to the membership itself in the form of the group's many social events. It is at the national convention, the focal point of LULAC life, where the web of dependence and the increased focus on solidary rewards is most evident.

By the late 1980s, the annual national convention had become heavily subsidized by industries and corporations seeking to market their products and improve their image in the Hispanic community. Floor space at the "trade fair" section of the national convention was quickly sold out as numerous industries tried to make inroads into the growing Latino market. One recent national convention boasted over 154 exhibitions from 71 government agencies or corporations who paid between $800 and $1,000 to advertise their goods (LULAC 1988b). More generous contributors are sorted into "gold" ($15,000), "silver" ($10,000), and "bronze" ($5,000) categories (LULAC 1987). Visitors to the exhibition room could find a wide range of food samples available from corporations as diverse as Church's Fried Chicken, Campbell Soup Company, and the Carnation Company, which actively promote their businesses and distribute free samples of their products. Their appeals were aimed at a general Hispanic audience, as conventioneers were urged to enjoy Coca Cola "y su comida favorita" (and your favorite food) and told that this Bud "es para Usted" (is for you).

Many of the solidary rewards derived from LULAC membership come during the state and national conventions. In turn, many of those benefits flow directly from the close working relationship the organization has with the private sector, as corporate monies find their way into other activities and events at the national and state conventions. For many, these annual events provide an opportunity to enjoy a subsidized vacation at some of the best hotels in the Southwest. The carnival-like atmosphere of these conventions comes complete with free food, beer, souvenirs, and music provided by the private sector. In 1988, the six-day convention featured an array of subsidized social functions. A partial list of the corporate-sponsored events at the Dallas convention included

1. LULAC Golf Tournament, Adolph Coors Company
2. Breakfast for delegates, Kraft Incorporated and General Motors
3. "Salute to Corporate America" luncheon, G. Heilemann Brewery
4. "National Hispanic Leadership" banquet, Dr. Pepper
5. "Salute to Hispanic Law Enforcement Officials," Southland Corporation
6. "Salute to Women" luncheon, Anheuser Busch
7. "Presidential Banquet," Miller Brewing Company
8. Delegate breakfast, Republican National Hispanic Assembly
9. Two formal dances, various sponsors
10. Two dinner banquets, various sponsors. (LULAC 1988b)

Solidary rewards constitute one of the most potent lures the organization has to offer. Membership in LULAC now carries with it a wide array of social events for its members to participate in. The district and state conventions held every year are multiday affairs which feature dances, banquets, and other social events. Most councils hold an annual Feria de las Flores (Festival of Flowers) to raise monies for the LULAC scholarship fund, a tradition started in 1947 by LULAC council 2 in San Antonio. The objections raised at the time by some group members who argued that their organization was not a social club (J. Rodríguez 1971: 4) are long forgotten. This attitude underwent a transformation over the years, and by the early 1970s these same councils were declaring that "fun and fund go together" (J. Rodríguez 1971: 7).

Solidary incentives have clearly become an important, if not central, aspect of LULAC's incentive system for its middle- and upper-income membership. The entire convention package of events for an annual convention can cost more than $250 per person. Although most of the convention events are subsidized or free, individuals who attend the national convention must pay their own room, board, and airfare. The final cost of such an event can amount to thousands of dollars, a price that dwarfs the $12 annual dues required for membership in LULAC. Furthermore, the social activities sponsored by LULAC during its national and regional conventions are reinforced by the friendship networks formed within the organization. Fun, recreation, and association have become powerful rewards for joining LULAC in the 1980s. Eduardo Morga (national president, 1977–1978) said of the national conventions, "I go to see people that I know, it's like a big family. We rejoice at each other's company. We're not monks, we don't ignore the reality of our humanity. It's a bonus, in addition to getting things done." He added that LULAC could do without its social functions only "if you want to break up the organization" (Morga 1988).

Conclusion

The League of United Latin American Citizens has had a long and complex history. From its beginnings in South Texas to the present, LULAC has symbolized the Mexican American middle class's battle for equal civil rights. LULAC's evolution followed the path of organizational development predicted by incentive theory literature. Through an understanding of the incentives offered to its members, one can gain an insight into what inspired its members to join and kept them active as well as the factors that led to its eventual bureaucratization. The major set of incentives offered to LULAC members during the first phase of its growth (1929–1945) came primarily in the form of group loyalty and idealism, the purposive and expressive rewards received through group activism. LULAC's ideological package continued to serve as the primary inducement to participation when LULAC's maturation was disrupted by World War II. The opportunity to reorganize after the war stopped a process that might have eventually led to the group's early decline or death. The end of the Second World War not only created a new political and social atmosphere conducive to change in race relations across the United States (Bloom 1987), but LULAC was given a new lease on life. The feeling among returning Mexican American GIs was that the time was ripe for change and that full assimilation into American life for their people was possible. Their activities marked a clean break with the politics of Mexico and with an attachment to Mexican identity.

LULAC's set of purposive incentives struck a responsive chord in the upwardly mobile Mexican American population of the late 1940s and 1950s. It is noteworthy that the group did not create a set of material rewards during this second period of organizational development. While the Mexican American middle and professional class stood to gain from improved race relations, the rewards derived directly through membership in LULAC were ideological and purposive. The effectiveness of these rewards was reflected in the energy and time LULAC members devoted to the cause. During the 1950s and early 1960s, all the time devoted to LULAC fund drives, litigation, and pressure tactics was initiated by volunteers who gave of their time and effort to advance a cause. The league did not pay its officers, lawyers, or anyone else acting in the name of the group.

These were the golden years of LULAC activism. Historical evidence indicates that LULAC membership not only gave the individual a political cause and ideology, but group norms reinforced the expectation that all members would become involved in its activities. LULAC members made great personal sacrifices fighting segregation and discrimination. Material benefits were not available through LULAC, and those who were part of these campaigns recall the feeling of satisfaction they received as a result of their efforts. One attempt made to provide some material benefits in the form of life insurance failed during the 1950s. As one former activist put it, LULAC members during the 1950s were "not going to receive anything, nothing in return" (A. Hernández 1985). An important part of LULAC's purposive and expressive rewards was that material rewards were not derived through group membership.

These incentives worked well for LULAC through the fifteen years following the Second World War, but they were not likely to form an effective survival strategy for the long term. As was noted in Chapter 4, the decline of LULAC as a viable activist organization came as a result of three interrelated processes. The first was the effect of time and the demands of civil rights activism, both of which took their toll on the core of activists who joined the group after World War II. A primary example of this process wearing on the willingness of individuals to give of themselves to a political organization came in the area of education, where LULAC was the most active. Although LULAC won many legal battles in the area of desegregation, San Miguel (1987: 134) found that the late 1950s was an era of increased resistance from the white community to LULAC's efforts to desegregate the public schools. LULAC and other organizations had established a number of important legal precedents, but the actual implementation of school desegregation was circumvented in areas throughout Texas and the Southwest. The resistance was so strong that LULAC and the GI Forum perceived further litigation to be futile. No further litigation in that area would be initiated by the group until the late 1960s.

The second factor involved in the decline of LULAC's purposive incentives was its value structure. The manner in which LULAC framed its primary goal of equal opportunity, its primary purposive reward, was crucial to the organization's decline. The issue of discrimination against Mexican Americans was a motivating factor in the establishment of the group, but its effectiveness as a purposive incentive waned over the years because many within the group no longer perceived it as a pressing problem. Scholars have documented the willingness of individuals to join political organizations to advance collective goals, but in the case of LULAC, its set of purposive incentives was a weak inducement to immerse the group in political conflict (Browne 1983; Moe 1981; Cigler and Hansen 1983).

The differential economic status between Mexican Americans and Anglos did not result in a long-term motivation to remain active in LULAC. The LULAC call to battle was based on a definition of racism as the denial of equal opportunity. The element of conscious choice was at work here, and the decline of LULAC was not brought about simply by exhausting its volunteer membership. Many members of the LULAC old guard were very conscious of their reasons for joining, and when they began to decrease their levels of participation in the late 1950s and early 1960s, it was because they felt they had accomplished the group's goals. Equal opportunity, traditionally LULAC's most powerful purposive incentive, was no longer an effective inducement for membership retention. Attempts to steer LULAC in the direction of increased membership participation at that time only served to dramatize the fact that purposive incentives no longer played a central role in the group's functioning. Previous attempts to engage the national organization in a political endeavor failed. Instead of rekindling the activist fervor of its earlier period the leadership reduced an already light burden of participation on the membership and began its dependence on outside funding sources for its activities.

Finally, LULAC's failure to develop a set of material rewards makes its decline as an activist organization more understandable. In the case of LULAC, its conservative political ideology speeded the unraveling of this once dynamic civil rights organization. Time and fatigue took their toll, but it can also be argued that LULAC's expressive and purposive incentives explicitly denied the propriety of deriving material rewards through group membership. Its history was one which focused on the removal of discrimination, not the provision of individually consumable goods. In its formative years as well as in the post–World War II period, the group explicitly emphasized that LULAC was not a springboard for the advancement of one's career or the enhancement of one's quality of life. The group was dedicated to insuring that the footrace of life was run on equal terms for all participants.

The failure to develop a set of material incentives was a major failure from the perspective of incentive theory. As time passed, membership enthusiasm for political involvement began to wane. It was during the early to mid-1960s that LULAC began to show signs of strain. But much as our model predicted, a new set of incentives, material and otherwise, was devised. An organization as old and

well established as LULAC was faced with the necessity of formulating a set of tangible rewards that would satisfy its existing membership base as well as attract others to the fold. A full assessment
of the impact the lack of material incentives had on the group
should take into account the upward mobility of the LULAC membership. As early as the late 1950s some LULAC members expressed
the belief that great strides toward achieving legal and social
equality between the races had been achieved, that their struggles
had born fruit.

The effectiveness of LULAC's purposive and expressive rewards
was directly related to the experiences of these individuals as they
completed their formal education and began their professional ca-
reers. What historical information is available about the early
LULAC members indicates that they were the economically advan-
taged sector of the Mexican American population. Scattered evidence on the economic status of LULAC members over the years
sustains the argument that one reason for their cautious and conservative approach to politics and intergroup relations stemmed from
the economic interest they held in preserving the institutions that
had favored them. Contemporary evidence on their socioeconomic
status is more conclusive and lends further credence to such an assertion. A survey of the membership in 1983 reveals that LULAC's
membership is better educated than the Mexican American population as a whole (see Table 1).

LULAC membership has its base in the middle and upper classes,
a fact that has led critics of the group to argue that rather than acting
as a progressive political elite, groups like LULAC became guardians
of the status quo (Acuña 1988: 324–325). While this charge may be
overstated, LULAC members are middle- and upper-class Mexican
Americans, people for whom the need for large-scale social change
is less compelling than it might be for the poor. This is a critique
that has been voiced by the group's contemporary leadership. Past
national president Tony Bonilla has charged that "LULAC still effectively represents the large, growing Mexican-American middle class
and is more interested in issues that pertain to them" (Bailón 1988a:
13A). Others have been less charitable. Past national president
Mario Obledo has lost faith in the ability of the group to bring about
much, if any, change: "When people ask why we have been active
for fifty plus years, hell I don't know. When an organization does
little of anything, it can limp along for a long time" (Obledo 1986).

Historically, material incentives derived through LULAC-sponsored activism have come primarily through increased educational
and career opportunities. But this benefit was not one that could be

Table 1. *Education and Income Data*
for Mexican Americans and LULAC Members

	Education	
	LULAC Members (%)	Mexican Americans[a] (%)
0–4 years	N/A	21
5–8 years	N/A	29
Some high school	8	17
Completed high school	16	16
Some college	25	13
Completed college	18	2
Some graduate school	11	3
Completed graduate school	21	
Other	1	
Totals	100	101*

	Income	
	LULAC Members (%)	Mexican Americans[b] (%)
Under $5,000	N/A	23
$5,000–$10,000	6	28
$10,000–$15,000	10	22
$15,000–$20,000	28	12
$20,000 and over	56	16
Totals	100	101*

Source: LULAC data, Boone 1983.

[a]Rodolfo O. de la Garza and Robert R. Brischetto. 1982. *The Mexican-American Electorate: A Demographic Profile.* San Antonio: Southwest Voter Registration Education Project, p. 7.

[b]Ibid., p. 9.

*Due to rounding of numbers.

limited to LULAC members alone. It could be argued that their most powerful material benefit, equal opportunity, was one expressly designed for mass consumption. Indeed, a central component of its ideological package stressed individual achievement and mobility, *not* group benefits derived through interest group pressure.

Given the high educational and income levels among LULAC members, it is not surprising that these professionals could do without health insurance policies, credit unions, cash discounts, and lobbying efforts, amenities which could be derived through more conventional professional associations. During the post-World War II years, LULAC provided a network for the budding Mexican American professional class. One reason many LULAC activists cite for joining the organization in the 1950s was that there were no others which gave them the opportunity to meet other well-educated Mexican Americans. LULAC was one of the few organizations in which rising Mexican American white-collar workers could become part of a professional network (Villa 1986; R. Bonilla, Jr. 1985; Armendáriz 1985). As former national president William Bonilla recalled, "[In 1953] I wanted to meet people and establish myself. I was 22 years old, the other organizations were for elites and they didn't accept Mexicans in the first place" (W. Bonilla 1986a).

As race relations have improved, the time for LULAC to play that kind of role for its membership has passed. An emerging set of professional groups for Latinos such as the Hispanic Chamber of Commerce, the Texas Association of Bilingual Education, Incorporated Mexican-American Government Employees (IMAGE), and the Hispanic Business Association serve those needs. Still, the organization has survived and without the aid of material rewards. But it has done this by seeking outside funding for its projects.

As an activist-based national organization, LULAC has reached the point of stagnation, but as a self-perpetuating entity, it has experienced dramatic success. LULAC evolved from a decentralized activist group into one that demands little from its members and is dependent on outside sources of monies to fund its activities. The unstable and marginally involved membership base became secondary due to the group's involvement in governmental and corporate programs. Thus, while the league's public profile grew in the mid-1960s and the group was involved in a wide range of political activities, these events occurred with decreasing mass participation, increased leadership innovation, and a heavy dose of outside financial support. The result was the creation of several related but independent agencies with tenuous or nonexistent ties to LULAC, each with an independent bureaucratic structure and professional staff.

This situation poses an interesting challenge for future leadership initiatives in the area of civil rights or discrimination. The administrations of the Bonilla brothers and Mario Obledo represented a phase in which LULAC's leaders presented their ideological beliefs through the media and advanced a liberal agenda. As was argued in this chapter, it was difficult to engage the rank and file behind many of these initiatives. The conservative, low-key approach of Oscar Morán was more appropriate to an organization with a middle-class membership which had also shown little inclination or ability to act in concert as a national pressure group. Morán's three years as national president of LULAC was critiqued by some as a conservative phase of the group's life, one that was conducted "in the corporate boardrooms." The suggestion is that with the proper leadership, the group could regain some of its momentum. These hopes were rekindled with the election of José García de Lara as LULAC national president in 1988. Recalling the vocal and energetic leadership of Ruben Bonilla a decade earlier, he announced that he was prepared to move the group forward and call upon "the grass roots or the rank and file of the organization to be involved in national issues" (Bailón 1988b: 14A).

For those in the organization who were tired of the conservative leadership of Oscar Morán and wished to see LULAC recapture its activist zeal, the election of de Lara was a welcome sign. He defeated the bid of a Republican challenger to head the organization and made it clear that in order to make a positive impact on the community, LULAC had to be more liberal and aggressive. "If we don't do that, we're wasting our time. We'd be a social club," he asserted (Cantu 1988). De Lara had previously established a record of activism. As Texas state director of LULAC, he had built a reputation as an outspoken critic of the Reagan administration's policies in Central America and of immigration reform. He initiated voter registration drives, filed affirmative action suits, and established a Western Union "hotline" through which LULAC members could contact their representatives in Washington over any issue concerning Mexican Americans (de Lara 1988). Cruz Chavira, director of LULAC district 15, claimed that when de Lara was the Texas state director, the response of the membership to LULAC appeals for activism "doubled" (Cantu 1988).

Chavira's claim about a doubling of activism among LULAC councils at that time is unsubstantiated. What appears to be true for the national organization is a gradual decline in political activism as the group matured. As Wilson (1973) found in his early study of civil rights organizations, purposive incentives are necessary to maintain the rank and file's enthusiasm and active participation. De Lara or any other leader who wishes to revive LULAC's activism will face the same organizational problems which have developed over the years, not the least of which is difficulty in maintaining member enthusiasm. To develop and coordinate the type of activism envisioned by de Lara and some of his political allies, the group's middle-class members will have to be prodded into giving their time, energy, and resources at a level not witnessed since the 1940s and 1950s.

In the case of this middle-class organization, altruism or ethnic-group loyalty has limited usefulness for prodding members to political action. However, this is not to say that ethnicity has no role whatsoever. On the contrary, the idea that individual members should work for the improvement of their less fortunate compatriots is touted as the raison d'être of LULAC. LULAC state and national conventions all center on a "theme," and a series of strongly worded resolutions concerning the continuing social and economic problems faced by Latinos are passed at each one. The organization produces numerous studies, position papers, and news releases which reaffirm LULAC's commitment to their resolution. LULAC has not initiated recent regionwide voter registration drives, sustained lobbying efforts at the local and national levels, large-scale campaign drives, or cooperative efforts with other national civil rights organizations. Nor has the group served as a source of money to fund Latino lobbying or political efforts. Given the economic status of most LULAC members, it is instructive that the relatively undemanding act of contributing money to a cause has not become a requirement of group membership. Indeed, the organization itself cannot command enough money from its members to keep it from constantly teetering on the edge of bankruptcy.

One way LULAC could revive its activist spirit would be to devise a new set of purposive and expressive incentives or perhaps by reinterpreting its existing "Aims and Purposes" in a radically different way. Doing so would require that it take on characteristics of new organizations—those at the first stages of organizational development. It would, of course, prove difficult to impose a new ideological vision on a group of individuals who are loosely tied to the group in the first place. On the other hand, LULAC has failed to provide its members with material incentives such as professional workshops, job training, licensing programs, or other individually consumable values. Providing these benefits might offer the necessary impetus to increased activism, but thus far they have not materialized.

Over time there has been a gradual decline in the number of demands placed upon LULAC members and a corresponding increase in the number of solidary benefits derived from LULAC membership. When organizations become entrenched in such an exchange with their members it is difficult to break the cycle. Even the liberal activist José García de Lara (national president 1988–) was forced to work with this enduring aspect of LULAC dynamics. Determined to implement a membership campaign, he suggested that one way to build a larger organization was to in effect lower LULAC's membership demands even further by creating an "affiliate member" status. He suggested that the cost for such a membership would be one dollar for an individual per year or five dollars for an entire family (de Lara 1988). When asked about LULAC's continuing need to reach out to the corporate world for operating funds, he acknowledged the problem while putting it in optimistic terms: "If we can generate enough money, maybe we can have a good paid staff to go after these issues. There's just too much work for volunteers to do" (de Lara 1988).

6. Conclusion

LULAC of the 1990s is dramatically different from the small, tightly knit group of individuals that came together in 1929. Once on the cutting edge in the battle for civil rights for Mexican Americans, LULAC has lost its predominant position in the community. Increased levels of education and economic mobility have broken the lower-class/ethnic bond, and an increasing number of newer, more specialized Mexican American organizations compete with it for members. Although discrimination against Latinos continues, LULAC seems unable to mobilize its national network of councils. Indeed, support for any nationally coordinated LULAC political initiative is so weak that it no longer has its central office in Washington, D.C. In early 1983, the office of the national president reported that the organization was in a financial crisis, and ordered that all travel be eliminated and all but three staff members be given a leave of absence (T. Bonilla 1983). The Washington, D.C. office closed shortly thereafter and, from that point on, the LULAC national headquarters would then be located in the hometown of the LULAC national president.

LULAC's continuing travails have several implications for the literature concerning organizational development and Mexican American politics. First, as incentive theory would predict, minority organizations are not immune from the process of bureaucratization. Although LULAC occupies a singular position in the Mexican American community, its failure to generate a set of material incentives has made it an ineffectual organization. LULAC's seventh decade finds it struggling with the same organizational problems it has faced since the 1960s: membership instability, the dominance of leadership, and a dependence on solidary rewards and corporate donations for survival. The fact that the largest nationally coordinated civil rights organization for Mexican Americans should find itself unable to act decisively on the social and economic issues facing the

Mexican American community is striking given the enormity of those problems.

Second, there is a limit to the time in which any group's purposive and expressive rewards can maintain the freshness and vitality necessary to make it an effective vehicle for social change. According to the stages of organizational life outlined in Chapter 1, these time periods come in the early stages of a group's life, but because of its unique history, LULAC had two "mobilization" periods, times when it could recruit and inspire its members to act with its purposive and expressive incentives. The first came at the time of its founding in 1929 to 1941. The second came after World War II, when returning Mexican American veterans revived the moribund organization, to the late 1950s. It should be noted that both of these periods were relatively short, twelve and fifteen years, respectively. Time, effort, failure, as well as success took their toll. As the incentive literature predicts, all political groups reach an end to their activist phase.

Third, if LULAC's experience is an indicator, the future of broadly defined civil rights organizations for Mexican Americans is coming to an end. Increased levels of economic and social mobility among Mexican Americans and the class differentiations it creates has made it more difficult for any organization to represent the entire Mexican American community. As more and more specialized Mexican American interest groups form, they bring a more narrowly defined set of purposive and expressive incentives to the organizational marketplace. While it can be argued that there is a continuing need for a Mexican American civil rights advocacy group, the proliferation of special interest groups representing the Mexican American people has continued unabated since the late 1960s.[1] The trend for these organizations is to focus on the circumscribed social and economic affairs of their members rather than groupwide concerns. Unlike LULAC's traditional agenda, the issues pursued by these organizations are diverse, class-based, and potentially conflictual (Márquez 1990, 1991; Reitzes and Reitzes 1987). Who is to say that the Comisión Femenil Mexicana, the Latin American Manufacturers Association, or the Republican National Hispanic Assembly will agree on any specific plan of action? LULAC has always claimed to rise above narrow sectarian issues and pursue a "Hispanic agenda," but a program that can encompass the social and economic interests of all Mexican Americans is becoming more and more difficult to define, much less implement.

Finally, organizations can survive if they find outside sources of income and provide minimal rewards to their membership and leadership. As was argued in the previous chapters, LULAC was able to maintain a minimal level of membership participation and interest by lowering the demands placed on the rank and file and shifting part of the costs of participation to the government and the private sector. The leadership, on the other hand, is a core of individuals who not only give more of their time and effort but who receive rewards of an entirely different order. As LULAC leaders, these individuals are able to oversee such programs as the LULAC National Educational Service Centers, Project SER, the various LULAC housing projects, LULAC social service programs for the elderly, and the LULAC Foundation. Occasionally they are employed by these programs, but more often than not their reward comes in the form of the satisfaction of overseeing, administering, or expanding multi-million-dollar government-sponsored social services.

These individuals also enjoy a high degree of visibility as community leaders. Although LULAC does not occupy the dominant position in the Mexican American community it once did, the mass media continue to seek out LULAC officials for commentary on Latino affairs. Few Latino political leaders have the stature of Henry Cisneros, Gloria Molina, or César Chávez, but because of their organization's history and stature, LULAC officials are considered experts on Mexican American politics by the Anglo community. The organization has, since the 1960s, served as a political pulpit for its national, state, and local officials. For example, the media has published the opinions of Ruben Bonilla when he was Texas state director and national president of LULAC on such issues as political appointments, the Ku Klux Klan, federal aid to cities, racism on campus, and discrimination in hiring. Through the skillful use of the media, Bonilla also brought pressure to bear on public officials by calling for investigations on such problems as police brutality and bias in the criminal justice system.[2] More recently, other top LULAC leaders have spoken out on issues such as high school dropout rates, judicial elections, school funding, and the enforcement of the Immigration Reform and Control Act of 1986.[3]

As was argued in Chapter 5, rewards the leadership receive for their service allow us to understand their reasons for participating and the limited input from the general membership. LULAC national presidents who have been most successful in having their opinions published by the media have been the organization's most liberal leaders: Tony Bonilla, Ruben Bonilla, and Mario Obledo. They understood the problems of unemployment, immigration, and poverty as going beyond the enforcement of equal rights or access and argued for aggressive and oftentimes partisan policy programs. What is revealing about LULAC's bureaucratic structure is the way in which Oscar Morán, a conservative Republican, was able to advance a personal agenda that was radically different from that of his predecessors. His terms in office represented a period of time in which Ronald Reagan's administration received little or no criticism from America's most prominent civil rights organization for Latinos.

There are clear limits to the leadership's discretion. In 1977, while Texas state LULAC director, Ruben Bonilla used LULAC's prestige and limited resources to influence the electoral process. He created a new organization, Hispanics Organized for Political Education (HOPE), an entity he hoped would become LULAC's "political action arm." The new organization was designed to work at the grassroots level, register voters, and educate them on the issues of the day and create a unified Mexican American voting bloc (McLemore 1977, 1979). The idea did not generate much interest among LULAC members, and the new entity quickly evaporated. In 1982, as LULAC national president, he tried once again to engage his organization in the political arena by amending the LULAC constitution in order to create a Hispanic political action committee (PAC) to raise money and lobby Congress on issues of importance to Latinos. The idea was voted down at that year's national convention.[4]

The Future of LULAC

LULAC has long been marginal to the political process, and a growing number of new Mexican American political organizations are taking up the task of finding solutions to problems facing the community. In Texas, for example, LULAC's traditional stronghold, the most effective grassroots organizing among Mexican Americans is not being conducted by LULAC but by the Industrial Areas Foundation. These small, mostly lower-income groups have allied themselves with the Catholic Church to form an effective network that coordinates its activities to resolve such issues as water service delivery to *colonias* (unincorporated suburbs), educational financing, and toxic waste dumping in the minority community. It has done so without a national office, elaborate yearly conventions, or corporate support, yet the oldest and most successful of these organizations has only been operating since 1974 (Reitzes and Reitzes 1987: 119). It is groups like these that do the exhausting day-to-day work of organizing among disadvantaged Mexican Americans and take their concerns to decision-making centers (Márquez 1990; Ortiz 1984: 564–577). While an analysis of their organizing principles and incentive structure is beyond the scope of this study, a cursory view of their activities suggests that organizing among disadvantaged

Mexican Americans can yield tangible results in a relatively short period of time.[5]

As other Mexican American groups have established their influence, LULAC continues to flounder. The late 1980s and early 1990s was a time when a series of scandals and personality conflicts rocked the organization and bitterly divided the rank and file. In 1989, it was discovered that $88,000 donated to the LULAC Foundation had been misappropriated. A number of checks were made out to "cash," and individuals withdrew money from foundation accounts for unauthorized purposes. In response to the revelations, the foundation's board, all former LULAC national presidents, were asked to resign, LULAC removed its title from the foundation, and the Internal Revenue Service was asked to strip the LULAC Foundation of its tax-exempt status.[6] The following year, the Texas state director of LULAC was removed from office by newly elected national LULAC president José Vélez. The president charged that fraudulent practices were used in the previous year's Texas state elections. After a national committee investigated the allegations, it was recommended that all Texas state elections be declared null and void. An ugly fight ensued during which the Texas state director resigned and a U.S. district judge appointed an acting state director.[7] Perhaps the most embarrassing event since the impeachment of Joe Benetes came in 1991, when the national president of LULAC and a group of other LULAC officials were accused of filing as many as five hundred fraudulent alien amnesty applications through an immigration services business (Paz-Martínez 1991).

Incidents such as these place a burden on an organization already preoccupied with maintaining its fragile bureaucratic structure. The scandals set off conflicts that pitted individual leaders and their supporters against one another, to the exclusion of other concerns. In a complaint initially raised in the mid-1960s, LULAC leaders noted that their members did little more than bicker among themselves and exchange personal attacks. At the 1990 national convention, the newly elected LULAC national president charged that instead of dealing with more substantive issues, LULAC chose to concentrate "on personal, in-house issues."[8] The leadership was also fearful that the strife would damage LULAC's public image with the corporate world. After his removal from office in 1989, the Texas state director of LULAC charged that "carping among LULAC officers is costing the organization thousands of dollars in corporate donations."[9]

The continuing interpersonal conflicts, obsession with internal politics, and dependence on corporate contributions have become a hallmark of LULAC's organizational life since the mid-1960s. But these problems do not foretell the imminent collapse of the organization. LULAC's center of gravity may not be political activism, but compared to the numerous crises and challenges it faced in the past, its current problems are minor in scope.

It is likely that LULAC will survive as an organization, but one where instability is the norm and old councils disappear just as quickly as new ones are formed. As was demonstrated in Chapter 5, the "chaos and stagnation" reported within LULAC's ranks has its roots in the group's weak incentive structure. But LULAC leaders often contribute to the turmoil. Because delegates from individual councils, not the general membership, elect state national leaders and each council, no matter how small, is allocated a minimum number of delegates, ambitious LULAC politicians have chartered dozens of new councils that in turn support their bid for higher office. The creation of great numbers of new councils by ambitious LULAC leaders has always been a source of controversy. In 1990, when the Texas state director of LULAC was removed by the national president, one of the allegations was that he fraudulently created a number of councils that would support his reelection bid. Similarly, the 1990 election of the LULAC national president was rife with accusations of vote buying and election fraud.[10]

It is undeniable that some LULAC councils do become involved in community and political affairs. While they are active, these councils engage in a number of political activities in their own communities ranging from local economic development, social services to the elderly, hiring practices, youth conferences, redistricting plans, and language issues.[11] However, the short lifespan of these councils makes it difficult to assess the sum total of their efforts.[12] This constant turnover of members is at the root of many of the councils' demise. Few councils establish the staying power of such branches as LULAC Council 1 in Corpus Christi or Council 2 in San Antonio, which have been active since 1929.

One research project that would shed light on the full extent of LULAC's role in Mexican American politics at the local level would be to document the degree to which the group's name and prestige is a political resource in itself. The lack of stability among local councils might mask a rotation of political activists who use the name and image of LULAC to engage in a series of projects and political conflicts only to disband within a few years. Given the short period of time individuals stay in the group, it is possible that LULAC has become an institution whose name is a resource and general political guideline that community activists can use to advance short-term political goals.

In any case, the national organization will continue to survive as it acquires corporate donations, dispenses solidary incentives to the rank and file, provides personal gratification for the leadership, and serves as a loose network for middle-class activists. Local councils will have to compete with the wide array of other organizations representing Mexican Americans for their time and allegiance, but LULAC membership does not preclude activism in other groups. Most of the activists interviewed for this study reported membership in a number of other political organizations, both ethnically based and mainstream, Anglo-dominated groups. While many expressed frustration at the limited potential of LULAC, all found it to be useful for advancing their own political agenda. Those in key leadership positions cited the importance of LULAC as a vehicle through which they could increase their personal political influence. Nevertheless, it is not their only form of political participation. LULAC's leadership core is made up of a group of dedicated and energetic individuals who use the organization and its resources as it suits their purpose. As one past LULAC president (W. Bonilla 1986b) observed, "Some of us have just begun to fight."

Appendix. LULAC Membership Estimates, 1951–1983

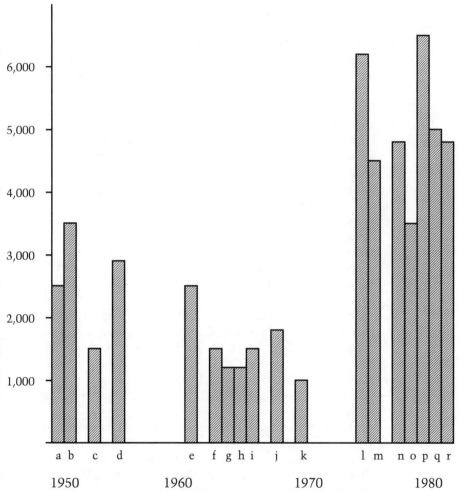

Note: Membership figures are estimates derived from LULAC financial statements. LULAC dues for 1951–1955 were $2 per year; 1962–1963 $6 per year; 1964–1979 $9 per year; 1979–1988 $12 per year. No information available for 1958, 1959, 1960, 1961, 1973, 1974, 1975, 1978.

a = 1951–1952. Report of the National Treasurer. League of United Latin American Citizens. Cash Receipts and Disbursements, June 24, 1951, to June 19, 1952. Income earned from dues = $4,956.

b = 1952–1953. Report of the National Treasurer. League of United Latin American Citizens. Cash Receipts and Disbursements, July 1952 to June 10, 1953. Dues = $6,600.

c = 1954–1955. LULAC National Office. Financial Statement, March 31, 1955. Dues = $3,187.

d = 1956–1957. "Minutes of the Texas Regional Convention." *LULAC News* (March 1957): 11. This rough estimate was derived from a treasurer's report that said it took $3,600 to run the national organization during 1956–1957. Dues = $3,600.

e = 1962–1963. San Antonio National Office. League of United Latin American Citizens Statement of Income and Expenses for the Period June 19, 1962, to June 25, 1963. Dues = $14,718.

f = 1964–1965. "1964–5 LULAC Budget." *LULAC News* 25, no. 10 (July 1964). Dues = $12,000.

g = 1965–1966. LULAC Operations. Statement of Cash Receipts and Disbursements as of June 15, 1965, to June 15, 1966. Dues = $15,000.

h = 1966–1967. LULAC Operations. Statement of Cash Receipts and Disbursements as of June 15, 1966, to June 15, 1967. Dues = $15,200.

i = 1967–1968. "Statement of Cash Receipts and Disbursements for the Period from July 1, 1967 through June 30, 1968." *LULAC News* 31, no. 12 (December 1968). Dues = $16,496.

j = 1969–1970. "Minutes from the LULAC National Convention of 1970." *LULAC News* 33, no. 3 (June 1971): 4. Dues = $18,489.

k = 1971–1972. Estimate. Interview with Paul Garza, Jr., January 17, 1986. Dues = $12,000.

l = 1976. Estimate. Interview with Manuel González, July 11, 1986. Dues collection rose dramatically because of the need to retire some of the debt incurred by Joseph Benetes.

The money represented advance dues payment. Dues = $75,000.

m = 1977. LULAC Foundation, Inc. Comparative Statement of Income, Expenses, and Change in Fund Balance for Years Ended December 31, 1978 and 1977. Dues = $50,000.

n = 1979. LULAC Statement of Operations, July 1, 1978, to June 30, 1979. Income estimate. Dues = $51,649.

o = 1980. LULAC National Office Statement of Operations, July 1, 1979, to June 15, 1980. Dues = $41,224.

p = 1981. LULAC National Office Statement of Operations, July 1, 1980, to June 30, 1981. Dues = $76,534.

q = 1982. LULAC National Office Statement of Cash Receipts and Disbursements for Period Ended June 30, 1982. Dues = $58,695.

r = 1983. Manny Villarreal. 1983. Memo to Tony Bonilla, January 21, 1983. Dues = $55,000.

Notes

2. Expressive and Purposive Incentives, 1929–1945

1. "La gran convención de la L.U.L.A.C.," *El Paladín*, May 17, 1929; "Los latino-americanos honraron a 'El Paladín,'" *El Paladín*, September 6, 1929. Other sources on early LULAC social events came from undated articles in *El Paladín* and the *Corpus Christi Caller*, as well as announcements of the coming events. All documents are available at the LULAC archives at the Benson Latin American Collection at The University of Texas at Austin.

2. Information on convention activities came from LULAC convention programs, 1930 through 1941. All documents are available at the LULAC archives at the Benson Latin American Collection at The University of Texas at Austin.

3. Estimates of early LULAC membership vary wildly. That 250 members attended the first LULAC convention was reported by the *Corpus Christi Caller* and *El Paladín*. The increase in the number of LULAC councils is documented in issues of the *LULAC News*. Later estimates of LULAC membership are derived from press reports on later national conventions. Edward Garza (1951: 22) estimated that LULAC in 1940 could claim 200 councils with an estimated 75 to 100 members per council. A membership count of between 15,000 and 20,000 would have made the organization larger than any other Mexican American group that has ever existed.

4. Mobilization and Transition, 1960–1985

1. Membership figures are estimates derived from LULAC financial statements. See the appendix.

5. The Politics of Survival

1. It should be noted that it is extraordinarily difficult to gain accurate counts or even estimates of LULAC membership over the years. The group has never kept very good records of its activities and most of its written materials have been lost or destroyed. Moreover, the contemporary organi-

zation has been secretive about its membership rolls, thereby making it difficult to estimate the size of its constituency. Reasonable estimates can be derived from the few financial reports and internal documents that exist (see Appendix).

6. Conclusion

1. González 1985; Caballero 1985; Schorr 1989; Zavala 1989; Smith 1990; Burek and Koek 1990; Davis 1989; Congressional Hispanic Caucus Institute, Inc. 1989; Rodríguez-Santos 1990; Mark 1990.

2. Mintz 1976; "Plodding Trial Irks LULAC," 1977; Harrigan 1977; "LULACs Seek State Probe of Hudspeth Inmate's Death," 1977; "LULAC to Monitor Courts," 1977; McLemore 1978; Villalobos 1978; Quintana 1978; Villalobos 1979; Gonzales 1979; Bartlett 1980.

3. "LULAC Challenges Judicial Elections," 1991; Olvera 1990; "Hispanics Protest Transfer of Houston INS Director," 1990; "LULAC Backs Tax to Fund Schools," 1991; Zamarripa 1989.

4. Sánchez 1982.

5. For the organizational strategy adopted by the Texas IAF, see Alinsky 1969, 1971, 1972.

6. Bragg 1989b; "Money Improprieties Cause Rift in LULAC," 1989; "LULAC Detaches from Official Board," 1989.

7. Hernández 1991a, 1991b, 1991c; "LULAC Squabble in Court," 1991; "LULAC Splits over Committee Head Selections," 1991.

8. "LULAC Leadership Showdown Is Today," 1990; "New LULAC President Pledges Unity after Vote," 1990.

9. Hernández 1991b.

10. "New LULAC President Pledges Unity after Vote," 1990; see Cárdenas 1984: 4.

11. Stamper 1975; Landon 1975; "LULAC Project Revives Memories of Medal Winners Slain in Korea," 1976; Hendricks 1979; Martin 1989; Márquez 1984; LULAC 1988a; Bragg 1989a; Martin 1989; "Del Río Endorsed by the Farwest Region Directors," 1989.

12. Data gathered by the organization reveal that LULAC individuals tend to stay in the organization for a short period of time. Forty-four percent of all LULAC members have served with the group five years or less and a full 75 percent have served ten years or less. See Boone 1983: 10.

Bibliography

Acuña, Rodolfo. 1988. *Occupied America*. New York: Harper & Row.

Alinsky, Saul. 1969. *Reveille for Radicals*. New York: Vintage.

———. 1971. *Rules for Radicals*. New York: Random House.

———. 1972. "A Candid Conversation with the Feisty Radical Organizer." *Playboy*. March.

Allsup, Carl. 1982. *The American G.I. Forum: Origins and Evolution*. Austin: University of Texas Press.

Altman, Barbara. 1982. *Memo to the LULAC Executive Board*. March 2.

Alvarado, Frank. 1934. "The Solution to Our Problems." *LULAC News* 3, no. 1.

Alvarado, Luis. 1961. "The Evils of the Bracero Program." *LULAC News* 32, no. 2.

Alvarez, Albert. 1973. "The Psycho-Historical and Socio-Economic Development of the Chicano Community in the United States." *Social Science Quarterly* 53.

Anaya, Rudolfo A., and Francisco A. Lomeli. 1989. *Aztlán: Essays on the Chicano Homeland*. Albuquerque: Academia/El Norte Publications.

Andow, Paul. 1963. "Civil Rights 'Quid Pro Quo.'" Unpublished essay, August 25. LULAC Archives, Benson Latin American Collection, University of Texas at Austin.

"Are Texas-Mexicans 'Americans'?" 1932. *LULAC News* 1, no. 9.

Armendáriz, Albert. 1953a. "Hello from Your National President." *LULAC News* 21, no. 1.

———. 1953b. "Hello from Your National President." *LULAC News* 21, no. 3.

———. 1967. "The Problem of Dues." *LULAC News* 39, no. 1.

———. 1985. Interview with author. August 3.

"Around the LULAC Shield." 1937. *LULAC News* 4, no. 2.

Avena, J. Richard. 1966. "Lulac Organizes Washington, D.C. Council." *LULAC News* extra, October.

Bailón, Gilbert. 1988a. "Group Picks Outspoken Leader." *Dallas Morning News*, July 11.

———. 1988b. "Members Hope Shift Won't Dilute Message." *Dallas Morning News*, July 11.

Barrera, Mario. 1979. *Race and Class in the Southwest.* Notre Dame: University of Notre Dame Press.
———. 1985. "The Historical Evolution of Chicano Ethnic Goals." *Sage Race Relations Abstracts* 10, no.1.
———. 1988. *Beyond Aztlan.* New York: Praeger Publishers.
Bartlett, Robert. 1980. "Hispanic Leader's Overture to Reagan." *San Francisco Chronicle,* June 20.
Bayes, Jane H. 1982. *Minority Politics and Ideologies in the United States.* Novato, Calif.: Chandler and Sharp Publishers.
Benetes, Joseph. 1974. *LULAC News* 36, no. 7.
Bloom, Jack M. 1987. *Class, Race, and the Civil Rights Movement.* Bloomington: Indiana University Press.
Bonilla, Ruben. Ca. 1979. "Carter Administration Record Regarding Hispanics." Unpublished essay. LULAC Archives, Benson Latin American Collection, University of Texas at Austin.
———. 1980. Memorandum to Tony [Bonilla] and Arnold [Torres], August 5. LULAC Archives, Benson Latin American Collection, University of Texas at Austin.
Bonilla, Ruben, Jr. 1985. Interview with author, May 23.
Bonilla, Tony. 1982a. Letter from Tony Bonilla to "Brothers & Sister LULACers," June 22.
———. 1982b. Letter to Hector Godinez, August 2. LULAC Archives, Benson Latin American Collection, University of Texas at Austin.
———. 1982c. Letter to Hector Godinez, August 10. LULAC Archives, Benson Latin American Collection, University of Texas at Austin.
———. 1983. Memorandum to Members of the National Staff of LULAC, January 24.
Bonilla, William D. 1964a. "United in Effort and Purpose." *LULAC News* 25, no. 10.
———. 1964b. "Minorities and Their Future." *LULAC News* 25, no. 14.
———. 1986a. Interview with author, July 12.
———. 1986b. Letter to author, July 21.
Boone, William A. 1983. "A Report on the Results of the LULAC Survey/ Assessment to the National Executive Board." Chicago: Martin, Boone Associates, March 18.
Bragg, Roy. 1989a. "Two Tales of Tension Sting West Texas." *Houston Chronicle,* November 19.
———. 1989b. "Scandal Rips LULAC Ranks from Within." *Houston Chronicle,* August 31.
Browne, William P. 1983. "Mobilizing and Activating Group Demands: The American Agriculture Movement." *Social Science Quarterly* 64, no. 1: 19–34.
Burek, Deborah M., and Karin Koek, eds. 1990. *Encyclopedia of Associations.* New York: Gale Research.
Caballero, César. 1985. *Chicano Organizations Directory.* New York: Neal-Schuman Publishers.
Calderón, Miguel V. 1974. "The SER Story." *LULAC News* 36, no. 4.

Camacho, Angie, and Nativo V. López. 1984. Letter to Mario Obledo, February 5. LULAC Archives, Benson Latin American Collection, University of Texas at Austin.

Canales, J. T. 1932. "Get Acquainted." *LULAC News* 2, no. 3.

———. 1937. "The Westward Trend of LULAC." *LULAC News* 4, no. 4.

Canamar, Henry. 1931. "Think." *LULAC News* 1, no. 3.

Cantu, Hector. 1988. "LULAC Chief Gets Vote of Confidence." *San Antonio Light*, May 16.

Cárdenas, Leo. 1984. "Little Book Wins Again." *Latino* 55, no. 2.

Casillas, Lucius. 1953. "E Pluribus Unum." *LULAC News*, August.

Chacón, Ramón D. 1984. "Labor Unrest and Industrialized Agriculture in California." *Social Science Quarterly* 65, no. 2.

Chandler, Charles Ray. 1968. "The Mexican-American Protest Movement in Texas." Ph.D. dissertation, Department of Sociology, Tulane University.

Chávez, Eppie. 1953. "Lulac and Your Community." *LULAC News* 21, no. 4.

Chávez, John R. 1984. *The Lost Land: The Chicano Image of the Southwest.* Albuquerque: University of New Mexico Press.

Chávez, Tom. 1961. "Editorial." *LULAC News* 32, no. 4.

Cigler, Allan J. 1984. "From Protest Group to Interest Group: Coping with Internal Factionalism and External Threats." Paper presented at the Annual Meeting of the American Political Science Association, August, Washington, D.C.

———. 1986. "From Protest Group to Interest Group: The Making of American Agriculture Movement, Inc." In Allan J. Cigler and Burdett A. Loomis, eds., *Interest Group Politics.* Washington, D.C.: Congressional Quarterly Press.

Cigler, Allan J., and John Mark Hansen. 1983. "Group Formation through Protest: The American Agricultural Movement." In Allan J. Cigler and Burdett A. Loomis, eds., *Interest Group Politics.* Washington, D.C.: Congressional Quarterly Press, pp. 84–109.

Cisneros, George. 1940. "LULAC and Education." *LULAC News* 7, no. 4.

Clark, Girard P. 1965. "First Job Placement Center Opened in Houston." *LULAC News* 27, no. 5.

Clark, Peter B., and James Q. Wilson. 1961. "Incentive Systems: A Theory of Organizations." *Administrative Science Quarterly* 6, no. 2.

Congressional Hispanic Caucus Institute, Inc. 1989. *Directory of Hispanic Organizations, 1989–91.* New York: Philip Morris.

Cortez, Carmen. 1958. "The Lulac Educational Fund Inc." *LULAC News* 26, no. 5.

Cortez, R. A. 1949. "A Monthly Message from the President General." *LULAC News* 15, no. 4.

Cruz, Tony. 1969. "Let's Leave Politics to Politicians." *LULAC News* 33, no. 6.

Cuellar, Alfredo. 1973. "Perspective on Politics." In Isidro Duran, ed., *Chicano Studies.* New York: Macmillan.

Dahl, Robert. 1961. *Who Governs?* New Haven: Yale University Press.

Davis, Ann, ed. 1989. *Washington Information Directory*. Washington, D.C.: Congressional Quarterly Press.

De la Garza, Rodolfo. 1932. "Who Are You?" *LULAC News* 2, no. 1.

De Lara, José García. 1988. Interview with author, October 3, San Antonio, Texas.

De León, Arnoldo. 1989. *Ethnicity in the Sunbelt: A History of Mexican Americans in Houston*. Houston: University of Houston, Mexican American Studies Program.

De Luna, Andrés. N.d.a. Speech to Monday Club. LULAC Archives, Benson Latin American Collection, University of Texas at Austin.

———. N.d.b. Transcript of radio speech. LULAC Archives, Benson Latin American Collection, University of Texas at Austin.

———. N.d.c. Transcript of radio broadcast. LULAC Archives, Benson Latin American Collection, University of Texas at Austin.

———. 1938. Transcript of radio broadcast. LULAC Archives, Benson Latin American Collection, University of Texas at Austin.

Del Olmo, Frank. 1984a. "Will We All Chug-a-Lug Now for Social Justice?" *Los Angeles Times*, November 1.

———. 1984b. "Building Bridges to Cuba." *Los Angeles Times*, September 13.

Del Río, Anita. 1986. Interview with author, July 11, Las Vegas, Nevada.

"Del Río Endorsed by the Farwest Region Directors Márquez, Romero and Vélez to Serve for Another Term as the National Vice President for the Farwest Region." 1989. Leaflet.

"Editorial." 1937. *LULAC News* 4, no. 1.

"Editorial." 1945a. *LULAC News* 12, no. 1.

"Editorial." 1945b. *LULAC News* 12, no. 4.

"Editorial." 1947. *LULAC News* 13, no. 9.

"Editorial." 1953. *LULAC News* 21, no. 3.

"Editorial." 1956. *LULAC News* 24, no. 1.

"Editorial." 1966. *LULAC News* 28, no. 1.

Eisinger, Peter. 1980. *The Politics of Displacement: Racial and Ethnic Transition in Three American Cities*. New York: Academic Press.

Flores, Willy. 1964. "L.U.L.A.C.—Past, Present and Future." *LULAC News* 15, no. 9.

"Ford Stock Hailed as Landmark in Public Ownership." 1956. *LULAC News* 23, no. 7.

Fraga, Luis R. 1980. "Organizational Maintenance and Organizational Effectiveness: The League of United Latin American Citizens." Paper presented at the Annual Meeting of the American Political Science Association, Washington, D.C., August.

Galván, Frank J., Jr. 1975. Interview by Richard Estrada, August 12. University of Texas at El Paso Institute of Oral History (Transcript #415).

García, J. Julio. 1973. "Letter from the Editor." *LULAC News* 35, no. 11.

García, Mario T. 1984a. "Americans All: The Mexican-American Generation and the Politics of Wartime Los Angeles, 1941–1949." *Social Science Quarterly* 65.

———. 1984b. "Mexican Americans and the Politics of Citizenship: The Case of El Paso, 1936." *New Mexico Historical Review* 59, no. 2: 187–204.

———. 1989. *Mexican Americans: Leadership, Ideology, and Identity.* New Haven: Yale University Press.

García, Richard A. 1978. "Class Consciousness and Ideology—The Mexican Community of San Antonio, Texas: 1930–1940." *Aztlán* 9.

———. 1983. "The Mexican-American Mind: A Product of the 1930s." In Mario T. García et al., eds., *History, Culture, and Society: Chicano Studies in the 1980s.* Ypsilanti: Bilingual Press.

Garza, Ben. 1929. Letter to Douglas O. Weeks, November 5.

Garza, Edward D. 1951. "LULAC: League of United Latin American Citizens." Master's thesis, Southwest Texas State Teachers College.

Garza, George J. 1947. "Means to an End." *LULAC News* 14, no. 3.

———. 1954. "Founding and History of LULAC." *LULAC News* (Twenty-fifth Anniversary Issue).

———. 1955a. "It Can Be Done." *LULAC News* 22, no. 11.

———. 1955b. Letter to William Flores, April 15. LULAC Archives, Benson Latin American Collection, University of Texas at Austin.

Garza, Paul, Jr. 1964. *LULAC News* 25, no. 14.

———. 1970. "President's Message." *LULAC News* 33, no. 1.

———. Ca. 1973. National LULAC Housing Consultant. "LULAC Housing Project Phase 'A' General Information."

———. 1986. Interview with author, January 17.

Garza, Tomás A. 1931. "Forward to Washington!" *LULAC News* 1, no. 3.

———. 1932. "LULAC: A Future Power." *LULAC News* 1, no. 7.

Girón, T. G. 1933. "The League of United Latin American Citizens." *LULAC News* 2, no. 7.

Godínez, Hector. 1961. "Message from Our National President." *LULAC News* 32, no. 4.

———. N.d. "Message from Our National President." Flyer, LULAC Archives, Benson Latin American Collection, University of Texas at Austin.

Gómez-Quiñones, Juan. 1978. *Mexican Students por La Raza: The Chicano Student Movement in Southern California 1967–1977.* Santa Barbara: Editorial La Causa.

Gonzales, Diana. 1979. "Groups Ask Close KKK Watch." *San Antonio Express*, December 16.

González, Albert. 1954. "Employing the Handicapped." *LULAC News* (Twenty-fifth Anniversary Issue).

González, M. C. 1930. "The Future of Our League Depends on How Seriously We Conduct Its Business." *La Verdad*, February 22.

———. 1932. "The Aim of LULAC." *LULAC News* 1, no. 8.

———. 1946. Letter to John J. Herrera, April 26. LULAC Archives, Benson Latin American Collection, University of Texas at Austin.

González, Manuel. 1986. Interview with author, July 11.

González, Sylvia, ed. 1985. *Hispanic American Voluntary Organizations.* Westport, Conn.: Greenwood Press.

Gordon, Milton M. 1964. *Assimilation in American Life.* New York: Oxford University Press.

Gutiérrez, David G. 1987. "Ethnicity, Ideology, and Political Development: Mexican Immigration as a Political Issue in the Chicano Community, 1910–1977." Ph.d. dissertation, Stanford University.

Hammerbach, et al. 1985. *War of Words: Chicano Protest in the 1960s and 1970s.* Westport, Conn.: Greenwood Press.

Hansen, John Mark. 1985. "The Political Economy of Group Membership." *American Political Science Review* 79, no. 1.

Harrigan, John. 1977. "3 Slain by Texas Police, Latin League's Chief Says." *Arizona Republic,* May 16.

Hendricks, David. 1979. "LULAC Candidates Forum Mixes Fiesta, Politics." *San Antonio Express,* April 1.

Hernández, Albert. 1954. "Hello from Your National President." *LULAC News* 21, no. 11.

Hernández, Alfred J. 1966. "A Message from the National President." *LULAC News* 28, no. 3.

———. 1967. "A Message from the National President." *LULAC News* 39, no. 6.

———. 1985. Interview with author, July 22.

Hernández, Andrés. 1938. "In Relation to Our Civil Liberties." *LULAC News* 5, no. 5.

Hernández, Daisy M. 1985a. Memo to All Regional Vice-Presidents and State Directors, January 11. LULAC Archives, Benson Latin American Collection, University of Texas at Austin.

———. 1985b. Memo to Arnold Torres, March 13. LULAC Archives, Benson Latin American Collection, University of Texas at Austin.

Hernández, José A. 1932. "A Nation's Real Wealth." *LULAC News* 2, no. 3.

Hernández, José Amaro. 1983. *Mutual Aid for Survival.* Malabar, Fl.: Robert E. Krieger Publishing.

Hernández, Raul. 1991a. "State LULAC Director Calls It Quits." *El Paso Herald Post,* February 22.

———. 1991b. "LULAC Squabble in Court." *El Paso Herald Post,* January 26.

———. 1991c. "50 El Pasoans Are Expected at State LULAC Meeting." *El Paso Herald Post,* May 30.

Herrera, John J. 1954a. "Lulac and the Latin American in Texas." Speech, LULAC Archives, Benson Latin American Collection, University of Texas at Austin.

———. 1954b. Letter to Luciano Santoscoy from John J. Herrera, reprinted in *LULAC News* 21, no. 12.

———. 1966. "Lulac Labor of Love." *LULAC News* 25, no. 3.

———. 1971. Speech, February 13, Rice Hotel, Houston, Texas. Houston Public Library.

———. 1985. Interview with author, May 26.

"Highlights and Resolutions of the 1966 LULAC National Convention." 1966. *LULAC News* 34, no. 1.

Hispanics Organized for Political Education (HOPE). 1980. Constitution and By-Laws.

"Hispanics Protest Transfer of Houston INS Director." 1990. *El Paso Herald Post*, March 10.

"A History of LULAC." 1974. *LULAC News* 36, no. 5.

Hoffman, Abraham. 1979. *Unwanted Mexican-Americans in the Great Depression*. Tucson: University of Arizona Press.

"Illinois Criticizes National Office." 1964. *LULAC News* 25, no. 7.

"Just Who Does Joe Benetes Think He Is?" 1973. *LULAC News* 35, no. 11.

Kushner, Sam. 1975. *Long Road to Delano*. New York: International Publishers.

Landon, Susan. 1975. "LULAC Will Now Support Bond Issue." *Arizona Journal*, June 12.

Lieberson, Stanley. 1980. *A Piece of the Pie: Blacks and White Immigrants since 1880*. Berkeley: University of California Press.

LULAC. 1939. The Constitution of the League of United Latin American Citizens. Adopted in San Antonio, June 3.

———. 1948–1949. "Roster of Active LULAC Councils 1948–49." Unpublished, typewritten report. Houston Public Library, Houston, Texas.

———. 1949. "Roster [of LULAC Councils]." Unpublished, typewritten report, October 9. LULAC Archives, Benson Latin American Collection, University of Texas at Austin.

———. 1952. "Roster of All LULAC Councils." Unpublished, typewritten report. LULAC Archives, Benson Latin American Collection, University of Texas at Austin.

———. 1981. "A Proposal to Institutionalize a National Office for the League of United Latin American Citizens." Unpublished, typewritten report. LULAC Archives, Benson Latin American Collection, University of Texas at Austin.

———. 1983. *LULAC National Annual Report*. Lulac Publication, Corpus Christi, Texas.

———. 1984. *Economic Analysis Review 1981–1984: Implications for Hispanic Americans*. Policy analysis paper.

———. 1987. "58th Annual Convention and Trade Fair." LULAC leaflet.

———. 1988a. Irvine LULAC Council 2064 Recognition Awards Program Fifth Annual Banquet, April 8, 1988. Program.

———. 1988b. "The Future Is Now: 59th Annual LULAC National Convention." Convention program.

"LULAC Backs Tax to Fund Schools." 1991. *El Paso Herald Post*, February 16.

LULAC Board of Directors. 1983. Meeting Minutes, June 30. LULAC Archives, Benson Latin American Collection, University of Texas at Austin.

"LULAC Business Development Program Announced." *La Luz* 5, no. 12: 21.

"LULAC Challenges Judicial Elections." 1991. *El Paso Herald Post*, January 19.

"LULAC Code." 1940. *LULAC News* 7, no. 11.

"LULAC Detaches from Official Board." 1989. *El Paso Herald Post*, September 10.
"LULAC District #1 Endorses Coors Trade Agreement." 1984. Press Release. LULAC Far West Region, November 16.
"LULAC Ends Support of Boycott on Coors." 1974. *El Paso Herald Post*, August 30.
LULAC Foundation, Inc. 1977-1978. "Corporate Statement of Income, Expenses, and Change in Fund Balance for the Years Ended Dec. 31, 1977 and 1978." LULAC Archives, Benson Latin American Collection, University of Texas at Austin.
———. 1978. "Notes to Financial Statements," December 31. LULAC Archives, Benson Latin American Collection, University of Texas at Austin.
———. 1980. "LULAC Foundation Chairman's Report," October. LULAC Archives, Benson Latin American Collection, University of Texas at Austin.
———. 1982a. "Report on Internal Accounting Control," December 31. LULAC Archives, Benson Latin American Collection, University of Texas at Austin.
———. 1982b. "Statement of Support, Revenue, and Expenses and Changes in Fiscal Balances for the Year Ended, Dec. 31, 1982."
———. N.d. "By Laws. LULAC Foundation." LULAC Archives, Benson Latin American Collection, University of Texas at Austin.
"LULAC in Action." 1954. *LULAC News* 21, February.
"LULAC in Action—Human Values, Unlimited: A Report on the Little School of the 400." 1960. Leaflet. LULAC Archives, Benson Latin American Collection, University of Texas at Austin.
"(LULAC) Income Received by Denver Office from Corporations." 1979. Mimeo. LULAC Archives, Benson Latin American Collection, University of Texas at Austin.
"LULAC Leadership Showdown Is Today." 1990. *El Paso Herald Post*, June 24.
LULAC National Educational Service Centers (LNESC). 1983. Progress Report.
"LULAC Project Revives Memories of Medal Winners Slain in Korea." 1976. *El Paso Times*, May 8.
"LULAC Report on Fact-Finding Mission to Cuba: Normalization of Diplomatic Relations Recommended." 1984. Prepared by Hispanic Fact-Finding Mission to Cuba, September 10.
"LULAC Review of Reaganomics: First Year, 1981." 1981. Position paper prepared by LULAC National Office. LULAC Archives, Benson Latin American Collection, University of Texas at Austin.
"LULAC Splits over Committee Head Selections." 1991. *El Paso Herald Post*, May 31.
"LULACs Seek State Probe of Hudspeth Inmate's Death." 1977. *El Paso Times*, July 8.
"LULAC Statement of Operations." 1978–1979. LULAC Archives, Benson Latin American Collection, University of Texas at Austin.

"LULAC through the Years: A History of Former LULAC Presidents." 1954. *LULAC News* 21, February.

"LULAC to Monitor Courts." 1977. *San Antonio Express*, December 24.

Machado, Mauro. 1928. "De ayer a hoy." *OKA News* 1, no. 3.

Machuca, J. 1965. "Report of the National Business Manager." *LULAC News* 26, no. 1.

———. 1975. Interview by Oscar J. Martínez, May 9. University of Texas at El Paso Institute of Oral History, Tape 152.

Mark, Samuel, coordinator. 1990. *Directory of the Hispanic Community of the County of Los Angeles*. Los Angeles: University of Southern California Hispanic Programs.

Márquez, Benjamin. 1989. "The Politics of Race and Assimilation: The League of United Latin American Citizens." *Western Political Quarterly* 42, no. 2.

———. 1990. "Organizing the Mexican American Community in Texas: The Legacy of Saul Alinsky." *Policy Studies Review* 9, no. 2: 355–373.

———. 1991. "After the Chicano Movement: The Emergence of Business and Professional Interest Groups in the Mexican American Community." Presented at the Western Political Science Association Annual Meeting, March 21–23, Seattle, Washington.

Márquez, Pauline. 1984. "LULAC Protests ABC's Hiring Practices." *Caminos* 5, no. 11.

Martin, Deborah. 1989. "LULAC Conference Gives Kids Wide Variety of Topics." *El Paso Herald Post*, October 26.

Martínez, Nick V. 1940. "Dependicitis." *LULAC News* 7, no. 4.

Martínez, Samuel R. 1982. Letter to Tony Bonilla, LULAC National President, September 22. LULAC Archives, Benson Latin American Collection, University of Texas at Austin.

McLemore, David. 1977. "LULAC Forms Political Group." *San Antonio Express*, December 4.

———. 1978. "LULAC Forming Task Forces." *San Antonio Express*, March 9.

———. 1979. "LULAC Pushes Voting, Politics as Ways to Power." *San Antonio Express*, May 18.

Mesa, Robert. 1939. Letter to Jeff Bell, November 24.

"Message from Dir. Pub." 1972. *LULAC News* 35, no. 2.

Miller, Lawrence, et al. 1984. "Attitudes toward Undocumented Workers: The Mexican-American Perspective." *Social Science Quarterly* 65.

Mintz, Bill. 1976. "LULAC Files Bias Action against Border Patrol." *San Antonio Express*, October 1.

Moe, Terry. 1981. "Toward a Broader View of Interest Groups." *Journal of Politics* 43: 493–543.

Moffett, Matt. 1986. "LULAC, Hispanic Advocacy Group Turns Away from Liberal Traditions under New Leadership." *Wall Street Journal*, March 19.

"Money Improprieties Cause Rift in LULAC." 1989. *El Paso Herald Post*, October 28.

Montalbo, Philip J. 1957. Letter to Felix Tijerina, May 27. LULAC Archives, Benson Latin American Collection, University of Texas at Austin.

————. 1966a. "The Latin American in Texas and the Southwest." *LULAC News* 28, no. 1.

————. 1966b. "The Latin American in Texas and the Southwest." *LULAC News* 28, no. 3.

Montejano, David. 1987. *Anglos and Mexicans in the Making of Texas, 1836–1986.* Austin: University of Texas Press.

Moore, Joan, and Harry Pachon. 1985. *Hispanics in the United States.* Englewood Cliffs, N.J.: Prentice-Hall.

Morales, Adrian. 1982. Letter to Sam Martínez of Adolph Coors Company, November 8. LULAC Archives, Benson Latin American Collection, University of Texas at Austin.

Moreno, José R. 1946. "The Price We Must Pay for Equality." *LULAC News* 13, no. 5.

Morga, Eduardo. 1988. Interview with author, August 21.

Morris, Aldon. 1984. *The Origins of the Civil Rights Movement.* New York: Free Press.

Mosqueda, Lawrence J. 1986. *Chicanos, Catholicism and Political Ideology.* Lanham, Md.: University Press of America.

Muñoz, Carlos. 1987. "Chicano Politics: The Current Conjuncture." *Year Left* 2: 35–52.

Muñoz, Carlos, Jr. 1989. *Youth, Identity, Power: The Chicano Movement.* London: Verso Press.

Naranjo, J. 1937. "Educating Our Latin-American Children." *LULAC News* 4, no. 7.

Navarro, Armando. 1974. "The Evolution of Chicano Politics." *Aztlan* 5, no. 1 and 2.

"New LULAC President Pledges Unity after Vote." 1990. *El Paso Herald Post*, June 25.

"Not the Same." 1957. *LULAC News*, June.

Noticias from the League of United Latin American Citizens. 1979. July 24.

Obledo, Mario. 1984. "National President's Activity Report." October.

————. 1986. Interview with author, July 10.

O'Connor, Karen, and Lee Epstein. 1984. "A Legal Voice for the Chicano Community: The Activities of the Mexican-American Legal Defense and Educational Fund, 1968–1982." *Social Science Quarterly* 65, no. 2.

Oliveira, Annette. 1978. *MALDEF: Diez años.* San Francisco: MALDEF.

Olson, Mancur. 1971. *The Logic of Collective Action.* Cambridge: Harvard University Press.

Olvera, Joe. 1984. "Cuba Trip Pleases, Disappoints LULAC." *El Paso Herald Post*, September 12.

————. 1990. "LULAC Chief Pledges to Cut Dropout Rate." *El Paso Times*, September 2.

Ornelas, Roberto. 1967. "The Mexican-American Reply to Stokley Carmichael." *LULAC News* 29, no. 9.

————. 1986. Interview with author, January 18.

Ortiz, Isidro. 1984. "Chicano Urban Politics and the Politics of Reform in the Seventies." *Western Political Quarterly* 37, no. 4: 564–577.

———. 1987. "The Reagan Agenda, Latinos, and the Future of American Politics." Paper presented at the Conference on Ethnic and Racial Minorities in Advanced Industrial Democracies, University of Notre Dame, Notre Dame, Indiana, December 3–5.

Paz-Martínez, Eduardo. 1991. "LULAC Leader Asks Feds for Courtesy." *Las Vegas Review Journal*, March 28.

"Pecos School Segregation Case Decision." 1954. *LULAC News* 21.

Peña, Eduardo. 1986. Interview with author, January 18.

Perales, Alonso. 1928. Letter to Ben Garza, June 22. LULAC Archives, Benson Latin American Collection, University of Texas at Austin.

———. 1929a. "The Unification of the Mexican-American VI." *La Prensa*, August 21.

———. 1929b. "The Unification of the Mexican-American III." *La Prensa*, September 6.

———. 1929c. "The Unification of the Mexican-American IV." *La Prensa*, September 7.

———. 1929d. "The Unification of the Mexican-American V." *La Prensa*, September 9.

———. 1930. Articles of Impeachment against C. N. Idar and M. C. González, March 5.

———. 1931. *El méxico americano y la política del sur de Texas*. San Antonio: Artes Gráficas.

———. 1978. "The Test of a Good LULAC Council." In *LULAC: 50 Years of Serving Hispanics*. Corpus Christi, Tex.: Baldwin Printing Company.

Perales, Leon. 1961. "Lulac." Leaflet. LULAC Archives, Benson Latin American Collection, University of Texas at Austin.

Pinckney, Alphonso. 1984. *The Myth of Black Progress*. Cambridge: Cambridge University Press.

Pinedo, Frank. 1954. "A Message from the National President." *LULAC News* 22, no. 2.

———. 1985. Interview with author, May 24.

"Plodding Trial Irks LULAC." 1977. *El Paso Times*, September 15.

"The Presidency." 1964. *LULAC News* 25, no. 9.

Press Release. 1980. American GI Forum of the United States, March 24.

Preston, Michael, et al., eds. 1987. *The New Black Politics*. New York: Longman.

"A Proposal to Institutionalize a National Office for the League of United Latin American Citizens." 1981. LULAC. Fall.

Quintana, Joe. 1978. "LULAC Examines Texas Police Violence." *El Paso Times*, May 20.

Quintanilla, Michael. 1985. "New LULAC President Sets Goals." *El Paso Herald Post* , July 1.

"Reaganomics: A Threat to Internal Security." 1983. Position paper prepared by LULAC National Office.

Recio, Federico. 1932. Letter. *LULAC News* 1, no. 8.

Reich, Michael. 1981. *Racial Inequality*. Princeton: Princeton University Press.
Reisler, Mark. 1976. *By the Sweat of Their Brow*. Westport, Conn.: Greenwood Press.
Reitzes, Donald D., and Reitzes, Dietrich C. 1987. *The Alinsky Legacy: Alive and Kicking*. Greenwich: JAI Press.
"Resolutions." 1953. *LULAC News* 21, no. 2.
Rhinehart, Marilyn D., and Thomas H. Kreneck. 1989. "The Minimum Wage March of 1966: A Case Study in Mexican American Politics, Labor, and Identity." *Houston Review* 11: 27–44.
Robles, Belén. 1985. Interview with author, May 26.
Rodríguez, Jacob I. 1952. "La Feria de las Flores." Unpublished essay. LULAC Archives, Benson Latin American Collection, University of Texas at Austin.
———. Ca. 1960. "Historical Background: LULAC Educational Fund, Inc."
———. 1965. "The Little School of the 400." *LULAC News* (April).
———. 1970. "A Declaration of Independence 1970 Style. A Declaration of Freedom from Racial Polarization and a Spurius [sic] and Unnecessary 'Search for Identity.' " Unpublished manuscript, July 4. LULAC Archives, Benson Latin American Collection, University of Texas at Austin.
———. 1971. "La Feria de las Flores: The Festival with a Purpose." Unpublished original script and narration.
Rodríguez, Jovenico. 1936. Letter to U.S. Senator Tom Connely, November 23. LULAC Archives, Benson Latin American Collection, University of Texas at Austin.
Rodríguez, Richard. 1965. "Here and Now." *LULAC News* 27, no. 5.
Rodríguez-Santos, Alfredo. 1990. *The Directory of 200: A Guide to Hispanic Organizations in Houston, Texas*. Houston: Aztlán Development Company.
Rosales, F. Arturo. 1983. "Houston's LULAC Council 60: A Case Study of LULAC Early Politics." Unpublished essay.
Roster of Active LULAC Councils. 1949. October 9.
Ruiz, J. J. 1932a. "Defense of the Mexican." Unpublished essay, February 12. LULAC Archives, Benson Latin American Collection, University of Texas at Austin.
———. 1932b. Notes, February 12. LULAC Archives, Benson Latin American Collection, University of Texas at Austin.
Ruiz Ibanez, M. 1966. "LULACs Approve Valley Strike Aid." *LULAC News* 24, October.
Salinas, Ezequiel D. Ca. 1930. "The Need for LULAC." In *LULAC: 50 Years of Serving Hispanics*. Corpus Christi, Tex.: Baldwin Printing Company.
———. 1937. "The Need for LULAC." *LULAC News* 4, no. 7.
———. 1939. "Our Americanism." *LULAC News* 6, no. 7.
Salinas, Gregory R. 1936. Letter to Louis Wilmont, August 13.
Salisbury, Robert H. 1969. "An Exchange Theory of Interest Groups." *Midwest Journal of Political Science* 13, no. 1.

———. 1984. "Interest Representation: The Dominance of Institutions." *American Political Science Review* 78, no. 1.

Salmon, Nick. 1961. "Our American Phenomena." *LULAC News* 32, no. 2.

Sánchez, Felix. 1982. "LULAC Rejects PAC Proposal." *Corpus Christi Caller Times*, July 5.

Sánchez, George I. 1940. "Americanism." *LULAC News* 7, no. 2.

———. 1949. "Special School Fund Report." *LULAC News* 15, no. 4.

Sandoval, Moisés. 1979. *Our Legacy: The First Fifty Years.* Washington, D.C.: LULAC.

San Miguel, Guadalupe, Jr. 1983. "The Struggle against Separate and Unequal Schools: Middle Class Mexican-Americans and the Desegregation Campaign in Texas, 1929–1957." *History of Education Quarterly* 23, no. 3.

———. 1987. *Let Them All Take Heed.* Albuquerque: University of New Mexico Press.

Santoscoy, Luciano. 1953. "Editorial." *LULAC News* 21, no. 4.

———. 1954. "Editorial." *LULAC News* 21, no. 10.

———. 1985. Interview with author, August 8.

Scharrer, Gary. 1985a. "LULAC President Reaches to Corporate America." *El Paso Times*, June 21.

———. 1985b. "New Administration Means Big Changes." *El Paso Times*, June 21.

Schorr, Alan Edward, ed. 1989. *Hispanic Resource Directory.* Juneau, Ak.: Denali Press.

SER Annual Report 81/82. 1982. Dallas: SER–Jobs for Progress.

SER Network Directory. 1985. Dallas: SER–Jobs for Progress.

"60th Attend LULAC California State Ball." 1984. *Latino* 55, no. 1.

Smith, Darren L., ed. 1990. *Hispanic Americans Information Directory 1990–1991.* New York: Gale Research.

Smith, V. Kerry. 1985. "A Theoretical Analysis of the 'Green Lobby.'" *American Political Science Review* 79, no. 1.

Sowell, Thomas. 1981. *Ethnic America.* New York: Basic Books.

Stamper, Janelle. 1975. "Possible Recall of Treasurer Explored by LULAC Council." *Arizona Journal*, April 3.

Stone, John. 1985. *Racial Conflict in Contemporary Society.* Cambridge: Harvard University Press.

Szymanski, Albert. 1983. *Class Structure: A Critical Perspective.* New York: Praeger Publishers.

Tafolla, James. 1927. Letter to Alonso Perales, December 16.

Taylor, Paul S. 1934. *An American Mexican Frontier.* Chapel Hill: University of North Carolina Press.

Tijerina, Felix. 1958. President Lulac Educational Fund, Inc. to the Board of Directors, Lulac Educational Fund, Inc., September 23. LULAC Archives, Benson Latin American Collection, University of Texas at Austin.

———. 1962. "Informe de la escuelita de las 400." LULAC Educational Fund.

Tirado, Miguel. 1970. "Mexican-American Community Organizations." *Aztlán* 1, no. 1.

Torres, Arnold. 1984. Memo to Mario Obledo, LULAC National President, LULAC Executive Director, January 20.

"Torres Resigns, Plans New Group." 1985. *Nuestro* 9, no. 5.

Treveno, A. M. 1937. "Around the LULAC Shield." *LULAC News* 4, no. 2.

Vara, Rudolph. 1984. Interview [by Thomas Kreneck], January 16. Houston Public Library, Houston, Texas.

Valdez, Frank M. 1969. "LULAC Housing Program." *LULAC News* 32, no. 3.

Valencia, F. 1932. "Editorial." *LULAC News* 1, no. 8.

Vásquez, Arturo. N.d. Financial Report 1966–68. LULAC Archives, Benson Latin American Collection, University of Texas at Austin.

Villa, Pete V. 1971. "Message from the National President." *LULAC News* 34, no. 2.

———. 1986. Interview with the author, July 12.

Villalobos, Ramón. 1978. "LULAC to Demand Evans Dismissal." *El Paso Times*, March 18.

———. 1979. "Mexican Americans Clamor for Hispanic Ambassador." *El Paso Times*, March 30.

Villarreal, Manny. 1983. Memo to Tony Bonilla, January 21.

Walker, Jack. L. 1983. "The Origins and Maintenance of Interest Groups in America." *American Political Science Review* 77, no. 2.

Weeks, O. Douglas. 1929. "The League of Latin American Citizens: A Texas Mexican Civil Organization." *Social Science Quarterly* 10.

"Wetback Roundup Needs Support of LULAC." 1954. *LULAC News* 22, no. 1.

Wilson, James Q. 1973. *Political Organizations*. New York: Basic Books.

Wolfinger, Raymond E. 1965. "The Development and Persistence of Ethnic Voting." *American Political Science Review* 59, no. 2.

Wright, Erik. 1976. "Class Structure and Income Inequality." Ph.D. dissertation, University of California, Berkeley.

Zamarripa, Leticia. 1989. "LULAC Lashes at Reform Law." *El Paso Herald Post*, July 8.

Zavala, Juan O., and Angela E. Zavala, eds. 1989. *Anuario Hispano-Hispanic Yearbook*. McLean, Vir.: TIYM Publishing Company.

Index